To Jack,

Best Wishes

Phil Bennett.

RUGBYWORLD
Yearbook 2012

Editor

Ian Robertson

Photographs

Getty Images

G2 entertainment

This book has been produced for G2 Entertainment Ltd
by Lennard Books
a division of Lennard Associates Ltd
Windmill Cottage
Mackerye End
Harpenden
Herts AL5 5DR

This edition first published in the UK in 2011
by G2 Entertainment Limited

EAN/ISBN 978-1-908461-31-5

Production Editor: Chris Marshall
Design Consultant: Paul Cooper
Printed and bound in Britain by Butler, Tanner & Dennis

The publishers would like to thank Getty Images for providing most of the photographs for this book. The publishers would also like to thank Fotosport UK, Inpho Photography, Chris Thau and Wooden Spoon for additional material.

100% ENGLISH

Crafted with locally sourced, 100% English ingredients from the heart of the Suffolk countryside.

BREWED IN BURY ST EDMUNDS SINCE 1799

A PROPER PINT

Aberdeen Asset Management is proud to support Wooden Spoon and wish them every success in all their upcoming events.

For more information please visit:
www.aberdeen-asset.com/sponsorship

GLOBAL ASSET MANAGEMENT

Contents

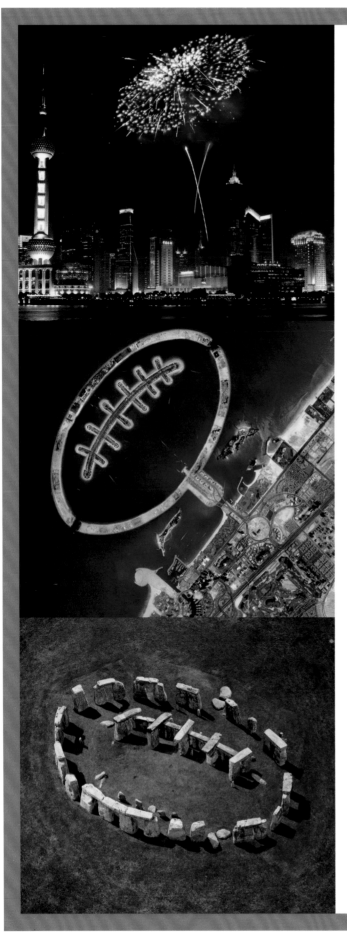

Supporting the growth of world rugby.

At HSBC, we're committed to the growth of rugby across the globe. We understand that the game has the capacity to connect different people, cultures and communities. Our investment in the sport spans from grass roots rugby right through to the highest level of the professional game. Which is why we are proud sponsors of the HSBC Asian Five Nations, the HSBC Sevens World Series, the HSBC Penguin International Coaching Academy and the British and Irish Lions Tour to Australia in 2013.

HSBC

The world's local bank

FOREWORD

by HRH THE PRINCESS ROYAL

BUCKINGHAM PALACE

HRH The Princess Royal,
Royal Patron of Wooden Spoon.

Since 1983, Wooden Spoon has been making a positive impact to the lives of disadvantaged children and young people throughout the British Isles. Wooden Spoon believes that all children and young people deserve the chance to live happy and fulfilled lives regardless of the challenges they may face. Wooden Spoon generates funds through the financial support of the local rugby community and its connected network and then donates the funds to much needed charitable projects throughout UK and Ireland.

Over the years, Spoon has donated in excess of £16 million and helped more than 500,000 children and young people through its charitable work. The projects have diversified from purely capital projects such as medical treatment and recovery centres, sports and activity areas, sensory rooms and gardens to include outreach programmes for children and young people in their communities.

These outreach programmes focus on tackling the growing problems of young people excluded from education, youth unemployment and youth crime. The projects use rugby as a sport to engage young people and build trust. Then, through a series of supporting programmes, help the participants exit to employment, apprenticeships or back into full time education. Rugby as a sport enjoys a tangible spirit and is perhaps uniquely placed to instil the values of hard work, fun, honesty, respect and teamwork in the individuals participating. In October 2010, I visited one of these outreach projects in Middlesbrough and was impressed by the enthusiasm of the young people attending and was encouraged by the results. These projects, now branded "Game On!" represent a new and exciting initiative for Wooden Spoon and I wish them well.

As a charity Wooden Spoon depends heavily on corporate and individual giving to achieve its charitable objectives. At a time when the demands on charities are growing, as Patron of Wooden Spoon, I invite you to lend your support to this charity that does so much to benefit the lives of our young people. With Wooden Spoon fundraising really is fun and hugely beneficial.

Anne

Wooden Spoon

The children's charity of rugby

Creating a stir for children and young people in the UK and Ireland

In the UK, one child in every hundred suffers from a lifelong disability that will profoundly affect his or her ability to lead a full and happy life.

More than 3.5 million young people grow up in low income households or live in an environment where they are subjected to poverty of aspiration.

At Wooden Spoon, we believe that all children and young people deserve the chance to live happy fulfilled lives regardless of the challenges they may face. Spoon harnesses the spirit and values of rugby to give disadvantaged children and young people in the UK and Ireland a chance to achieve their full potential in life.

Who we are:

Wooden Spoon is a children's charity founded in 1983 that is dedicated to helping underprivileged children and young people all over the UK and Ireland to live happier, richer lives. We partner with the UK rugby community, receiving invaluable support for our activities and the opportunity to raise awareness of the work we do. In doing so, we involve some of the UK's top sporting role models in making a difference in the lives of young people in need. We comprise over 40 regional volunteer committees as well as a central national team and we boast more than 10,000 members across the UK and Ireland. The regional committees undertake local fundraising activities and ensure that the money is spent on projects in their community so that the benefit of our work is always immediate, visible and lasting.

During our first 25 years, over half a million young people benefitted from more than £15 million of charitable support thanks to the efforts of our staff and volunteers. We are proud of our legacy, the work we do, and our ambitious plans for the future.

www.woodenspoon.com

Our vision

Wooden Spoon exists to make a positive impact on the lives of disadvantaged children and young people through our commitment to quality charitable work.

" We take tremendous pride in the professionalism, efficiency and the 'can-do' attitude of our volunteers who make so much of our work possible."

Jason Leonard OBE, Lead Ambassador of Wooden Spoon

What we do

We organise our own fundraising initiatives, raise the money and spend it where it is most needed. Over the years, our donations have diversified from purely capital projects such as medical treatment and recovery centres, sports and activity areas, sensory rooms and gardens, playgrounds and hydrotherapy pools to include outreach programmes for kids in their communities.

Some of our noteworthy projects

Wooden Spoon has funded hundreds of projects throughout the UK and Ireland. The following is a small but representative sample illustrating the scope and scale of Spoon's support for disadvantaged children and young people.

Children with cancer and leukaemia advice and support for parents (CCLASP)

Spoon donated £27,000 to pay for the refurbishment of a holiday respite cottage in Perthshire providing short-break holidays for children and their families.

Southwark Tigers

The Southwark Tigers began as a pilot project between Spoon, the RFU and Southwark Council to provide much needed activities for young people in an area of significant deprivation. By creating an opportunity for the young people of the community to play rugby, Spoon engaged young people in positive pastimes in an area that topped the national league tables for childhood obesity and teenage pregnancy.

Maesmarchog Primary School

The Special Needs Unit of this small village school in the Rhondda Valley received £20,000 from Spoon that funded the construction of a purpose-built playground for children with a range of autistic and behavioural learning difficulties.

Ace Centre

The ACE Centre in Oxford (Aiding Communication and Education) supports children with complex physical and communication disabilities. The centre was built in the grounds of the Nuffield Orthopaedic Hospital with the help of a £300,000 donation from Spoon. Here children are catered for with specific equipment and systems to help them communicate with parents, teachers and friends.

The ACE Centre is also involved in developing Stargaze, a breakthrough technology that tracks eye movements to help the severely disabled communicate and express themselves. Leicester and England U21 rugby player Matt Hampson and Spoon are proud to be involved in ongoing fundraising for the development and purchase of these systems.

The ABLE Partnership

£34,000 from Spoon paid for the construction and equipping of three greenhouses with advanced irrigation systems for growing a variety of foods. This is part of an extensive programme of education and training leading to the rehabilitation of socially and educationally excluded young people in Yorkshire.

The Cedar Foundation

Spoon donated £120,000 to this Foundation, which provides an extensive range of facilities to the disabled children of Northern Ireland, for the rebuilding and re-equipping of a building that is now the Foundation's flagship operation in the Province.

Game On!

Game On! is an innovative social investment programme designed to reduce the number of young people from socially challenging areas falling into long-term unemployment or a life of crime.

Harnessing the power and values of rugby, Game On! encourages positive behaviour change, builds confidence and raises aspiration levels amongst disadvantaged and disillusioned young people. Its unique programme of education and training will help 16-19 year-olds from deprived backgrounds into full-time education, apprenticeships, employment and long-term volunteer work.

A true "Big Society" programme, Game On! combines private sector sponsorship with substantial public funding to forge a sustainable social partnership that will help significantly improve the lives of young people across the UK.

What events do we run?

Spoon fundraisers

Spoon's volunteer committees organise hundreds of events every year including fundraising dinners, golf events, rugby matches, balls and other assorted events that allow us to raise money and attract the attention of potential supporters. These events also offer Spoon members the chance to contribute directly and network. Much of our impressive growth of members and sponsors is directly related to our event activity.

Spoon Challenges:

A series of physical challenges that occur across the UK where people can get involved and raise money for Spoon. Events include:

Great Lakeland Challenge

The longest, highest and steepest challenge. Participants kayak England's longest lake, cycle England's steepest passes and conquer England's highest peak - all in less than 12 hours.

Four Peaks Challenge

Our most successful and well-known challenge. Participants climb four of the highest mountains in Scotland, England, Wales and Ireland, a total of 14,000 feet and drive the 1,900 miles between them - all within 48 hours.

London Marathon

Wooden Spoon have 15 coveted Gold Bond places for the London Marathon. Run 26.2 miles for Wooden Spoon in the World's biggest marathon.

End 2 End Cycle Challenge

One of our most taxing challenges, participants hit the roads on two wheels to cycle the length of the UK from John O'Groats to Land's End, covering more than 850 miles in only 7.5 days.

Wooden Spoon Lead Ambassador

Our Lead Ambassador is Jason Leonard OBE, England's most capped player and World Cup winner. Jason is not only a testament to the sporting values of rugby, but he credits his involvement with rugby at a young age with transforming his life for the better. Having gained so much from playing a sport he loves, Jason uses his voice and influence to develop Wooden Spoon's work and help the less fortunate.

Wooden Spoon Ambassadors

Wooden Spoon enjoys the support of numerous rugby legends and industry leaders who contribute their time and energy to raise awareness of Spoon's activities and help us to generate funds.

Sporting Partners

Wooden Spoon enjoys strong relationships with a variety of clubs, league associations and governing bodies to achieve our common goal of giving back to the community while using sport as a way to improve the quality of life for young people.

Our Royal Patron

Our Royal Patron is HRH The Princess Royal who gives generously of her time.

Our Rugby Patrons

The RFU, WRU, SRU, IRFU, RFL all support us in our charitable work.

Corporate Partners

Wooden Spoon has the generous support of a number of companies whose contributions enable us to change the lives of more young people in a variety of ways.

Wooden Spoon
The children's charity of rugby

41 Frimley High Street, Frimley, Surrey, GU16 7HJ
Tel: 01276 410 180 Fax: 01276 410 181 Email: charity@woodenspoon.com
www.woodenspoon.com • www.spoonchallenges.com

Charity Registration No. 326691
(England & Wales)
and SC039247 (Scotland)

COMMENT
& FEATURES

Fiat Justitia Et Ruant Coeli

by PAUL STEPHENS

'Dismissals are usually forced on underperforming coaches. It was the only time in anyone's memory that an RFU chief executive was led to the exit'

In 1995 the International Rugby Football Board (IRFB) called two meetings, one in Paris, the other in Tokyo. The Rugby Football Union (RFU) were represented by John Jeavons-Fellows and Peter Brook. Their brief was to sign nothing and not allow rugby union to be sold to a professional group, whose only avowal was to make a profit on a game which for a century or more had grown into one of the great success stories of world sport, bound by amateurism as an unfettered and unchallenged belief.

The return from those meetings had unwanted consequences for Brook and Jeavons-Fellows, not to mention the RFU and the game as a whole. Although there had been no warrant to sign anything and there had been nothing as sordid as a vote on the subject, the International Rugby Football Board had their way and the game went professional. If they had fulfilled their obligations and insisted upon a vote, and if Brook and Jeavons-Fellows had given the lead which England had provided since the days when they alone controlled the IRFB, a majority of threequarters would have been necessary to abandon amateurism. Fifteen votes from 20. That was unattainable.

Until those fateful days 16 years ago, the IRFB's first commandment had been carved in stone: 'No person is allowed directly or indirectly to receive payment, benefit or other material reward for taking part.' The Tokyo and Paris meetings will go down in history as the most remarkable article in sporting history, particularly as the two RFU members had been mandated to oppose payment of any kind for actually playing the game. This must rank as one of the most astonishing pieces of procedural manipulation in rugby legend. From then on, this meant that truck drivers, shop assistants and roofing contractors could meet the clergy and company directors on equal playing terms. It also allowed the RFU to sanction those who had taken part in rugby league to move to rugby union. The game of rugby union in England went officially open in 1995. It was no longer hidebound by the amateur ethos. For the risk takers there was the opportunity to make some money; plenty of money for those willing to extend the risk element.

This is now mere history. Few under the age of 25 will be able to recall the amateur days. Apart from the unique structure and widespread allure of amateur rugby union, there was the fascination of the game with its distinct fellowship. This has gone, to be replaced by sponsorship, television and money, together with a lack of certainty. But there is no turning back the clock and we must make the best of it, bullion and all.

But have we not overlooked what happened during the summer of 2011, when rugby football showed a novel willingness to accept the unlearned lessons from six years previously, when Martyn Thomas was elected chairman of the Rugby Football Union? Thomas' first announcement was to tell those interested and ready to listen, 'My first duty is to help deliver a successful England. For this to happen the Premiership clubs must nurture and bring on players who are qualified to play for England. There is a determination at the RFU not to cover over our problems with anymore sticking plaster.' The key word in this brief effusion is *problems*. Six years into his chairmanship Thomas was almost suffocated by problems.

If you're sitting tight, maybe with a stiff drink in hand, I will attempt to explain. Firstly let me remind you of the names of the principal contestants in the furore. Thomas was central to the outcome. Next came His Honour Judge Jeff Blackett QC, the co-opted RFU disciplinary officer. Then there was John Steele, who had taken over from Francis Baron as the chief executive. Not to be overlooked is the name of Cliff Brittle, who briefly made the headlines, though for all the wrong reasons. There were others with bit parts, such as council member Alex Murphy.

The Rugby Football Union had been down this way before, when they called a Special General Meeting in Birmingham. Present were some 800 delegates who were balloted to decide if John Jeavons-Fellows, the RFU's chosen candidate, or Cliff Brittle should be elected to become chairman of their executive committee. At the end of a chaotic afternoon 16 years ago, with a long delay to count proxy votes, Brittle had emerged the winner by 647 votes to 332.

They apparently have remembered nothing from the Brittle Affair, or that Brittle sought legal action when the RFU commissioned Gerald Butler, a High Court judge, to investigate the way he was running the union. Butler was highly critical of Brittle's shortcomings, which the RFU man chose to overlook; Brittle was supported by Thomas, who was then chairman of the Reform Group and who led a lengthy cast of Brittle supporters. Brittle lasted just two years after his election before handing on to Brian Baister. It was an episode in the union's history marked by a lack of distinction, and one they would probably rather forget. If only they could.

The politically astute Thomas, who defeated Jack Rowell for the chairmanship in 2005, is a celebrated survivor and – with the notable support of the RFU powerbrokers, Fran Cotton and Bill Beaumont – had moved onwards and upwards by 2011. In what seemed like the blink of an eye, the RFU were without a chief executive; they had no finance officer, head of human resources, director of performance. Thomas, meanwhile, who had been on some £30,000 per year as chairman of the management board, was now on £350,000 as acting chief executive officer, and at the time of writing

was set to become the chair of the 2015 England RWC Committee, on £150,000. Not a bad emolument for one who had moved house close to Pendine Sands in far west Wales, where Donald and Sir Malcolm Campbell had performed as speed kings.

The monstrous infighting which characterised the dismissal of Steele and the quarrelling between Thomas and Blackett has been central to the hideous news emerging imprudently from Twickenham. Thomas was initially in support of John Steele as Baron's successor as chief executive of the RFU. Steele, bless him, was only in office for nine months when he was sent packing by all the nonsense that he had inherited. At the

LEFT Martyn Thomas, acting chief executive of the RFU – and chairman from April 2005 until he stood down in July 2011.

LEFT John Steele took over as chief executive of the RFU in September 2010 but by mid-June 2011 he was gone. His departure was triggered by his handling of the recruitment of a performance director. Steele, a former player and coach at Northampton and an erstwhile chief executive of UK Sport, left following a vote of no confidence by the RFU board.

root of the problem facing the RFU council was the opprobrium heaped on the unfortunate Steele for his handling of the recruitment process for the performance director's role after a change in the job description to exclude working with the senior England team, only to be faced with an embarrassing climbdown two days later. Steele was also involved in cancelling an interview with Sir Clive Woodward for the performance post, without setting a fresh date. Dismissals are usually forced on underperforming coaches. It was the only time in anyone's memory that an RFU chief executive was led to the exit.

Jeff Blackett, having considered his position after receiving the threat of a writ from Thomas for defamation during the Steele interlude, decided not to step down; instead Blackett will attempt to reform the beleaguered governing body from within. The board of directors survived a vote of no confidence at the AGM despite a damning 52-page report on the union, which recommended their removal. A significant number agreed to support a vote, which would have forced the directors to quit en bloc. Blackett went on record by revealing, 'I felt that my integrity had been impugned. The whole episode has impacted on me personally more than I expected. This together with the media attention caused me to question whether it was damaging the RFU, myself and my family by remaining as the disciplinary officer.'

The report made uncomfortable reading for Thomas, but more so for the RFU, raising the question of what next. Inevitably there were those not minded to accept the decisions of Thomas or Blackett. One such was Alex Murphy, who coincidentally had been appointed to the council by Thomas' area of Notts, Lincs & Derby and who was the first councillor to openly declare his intention to stand as chairman of the board. Murphy first declared he was against the selection procedure in 2010 and was investigated by a company approved and hired by the RFU after he claimed that the governing body had lost touch with the game's ethos. Somehow, I rather think Murphy was right. If he wasn't then the words of William Watson (1559-1603) should ring true: *Fiat Justitia et Ruant Coeli*. Let justice be done though the heavens fall.

Releasing the Pressure
Why Coaches Let Off Steam
by MICK CLEARY

'No wonder directors of rugby get uptight. They need a release valve. Their jobs are on the line, so too those of their players, if the team should lose'

We expect blood and thunder on the field of play, aggressive antics that occasionally spill over into trouble, to be sorted by the man in the middle or the citing officer sitting in some faraway darkened room. The bad boys are brought to book and sentences are dished out, many of them punitive, so much so that most everyone believes that the game has never been cleaner.

So is that why there is so much more focus on the off-field behaviour of coaches such as Brendan Venter, Richard Cockerill and Michael Cheika, the last-mentioned once of Leinster and now of Stade Francais? All three of them have found themselves embroiled in issues over the last few years, and all of them have had their collars felt by disciplinary officers to varying degrees.

Does this mean that rugby is on an inevitable decline, hurtling down the pathway that soccer took many years ago to the point now where you'd drop down in a dead faint if you heard a Premier League leading light admit that, yes, his man did handle the ball in the penalty area, and, yes, it was a complete disgrace that his midfielder had not been sent off for that vicious hack-down on the opposition striker? And as for the ref, well, wonderful wasn't he, very balanced, very correct in his decisions even if they went against us: there's got to be a man in the middle and his decision has to be final; it's about time we all recognised and respected that. No, I can't hear them saying such things either.

There is a depressing ring to such sentiments, and you can even hear some Premiership directors of rugby beginning to mouth those self-same, self-serving platitudes. Yet for the most part, they don't. There is more constraint, more tolerance, more empathy with the sport as a whole and with the difficulties of refereeing. Now, that doesn't mean that refs should be exempt from criticism. I've always taken issue with those in authority who insist that refs should not be held to public account, even if it is only by means of explaining decisions to the media afterwards. That refs are not subject even to this level of accountability is ridiculous. They should be obliged to tell the media – that is, you the public – why they awarded a particular penalty or sent someone to the sin-bin. Of course, if you're prepared to shell out a few quid for a Ref!Link or some such at Twickenham or the Millennium then you can pay to hear on-field explanations. That degree of interaction ought not to be subject to a commercial transaction. And that's talking about a bare minimum level of scrutiny.

No wonder directors of rugby get uptight. They need a release valve. Their jobs are on the line, so too those of their players, if the team should lose. Now, my belief is that if there has been an honest-to-goodness cock-up by the ref, perhaps because he was unsighted or simply because he boobed, then most directors of rugby would be even-handed enough to accept that such things happen. After all, players make mistakes. And, whisper it gently, even journalists, too.

The powers that be at Twickenham will tell you that there is a procedure for complaint, that directors of rugby can air grievances and get feedback from refereeing managers. All very well, but it's often too late and too far removed from the sharp end. What about those who've paid good money to come through the turnstiles? Where is their explanation, where is the duty of responsibility to them? They deserve to hear why decisions have been made.

It's my view that one of the reasons that directors of rugby sound off is simply because refs are cocooned away. Of course there has to be some sort

---

LEFT In July 2011, Michael Cheika, director of rugby at Stade Français, was fined a total of 20,000 Euros – with 10,000 suspended for two years – as a result of behaviour towards match officials and an ERC employee at the Amlin Challenge Cup final in May of that year. Both Cheika and the plaintiffs were granted the right to appeal.

ABOVE Brendan Venter (second from left in the back row), then director of rugby at Saracens, watches his team against Northampton in the semi-finals of the 2009-10 Guinness Premiership. He has been in hot water over comments about match officials and also received a ten-week ban for 'provocative and inappropriate gestures and comments' aimed at Leicester supporters at Welford Road in May 2010.

of distance kept between refs and directors of rugby in the potentially heated aftermath of a match. You don't want coaches headed into a ref's changing room. That's why an immediate forum for giving views – that is, to the media – ought to be provided.

Refs insist that they are accountable, that if they make errors they will drop down the rankings and not get the top games. Fair enough. It's match day, though, that matters, and that is when they should be heard as well as seen.

There are other issues that need addressing at games, principal among them that of where coaches should sit. They used to be in the touch-line dugout, but in order to try and control the congestion that occurs there, coaches were persuaded to take to the stands. In fact, for a rugby coach, there's a better view from the elevated position. He can see the shape of the field, the alignment of the attacks, the formation of the defences and the potential fault lines in opposition ranks. Quite whether the coaches would have taken themselves away from the touch line if there were no such thing as walkie-talkies is another matter. As it is, they can spot what's going on and instruct their platoon of helpers on the sideline to get a message to the players. Perhaps that's the answer – no contact at all between bench or coach and the players. Let them work it out for themselves.

What most certainly does need to come to pass is for coaches to be given a proper area in which to sit. It's no good putting them in amongst the general public as happens, for example, at Leicester. Even though Venter got himself entangled in all sorts of shenanigans last year when Saracens were in town, eventually copping a lengthy RFU ban that ruled him out of attending the Premiership final at Twickenham, Leicester have not significantly changed their set-up. It's time they did, along with all their Premiership colleagues.

Coaches are too exposed. As a player, Cockerill displayed the rawness of his emotions at every turn, and he is no different now as a director of rugby. To his credit he is not scheming or manipulative or contrived. He calls it as he sees it. Unfortunately he calls it too often. If he were behind a window in a dedicated area for coaches along the lines of a corporate hospitality box, then there would be no issues. He could rant and rave to his heart's content, just as long as there were no lip-readers outside looking in.

The stakes have upped in professional rugby: bigger crowds, greater rewards, more intrusive TV cameras. Let's not worry unduly if one or two coaches occasionally fire off. There is so much to admire in professional rugby. Players are far better behaved on and off the field than ever they were. We all worship at the stories told on the after-dinner circuit, laugh ourselves silly at tales of late-night high jinks and pianos tumbling out of hotel windows. However, if those sorts of things happened these days, then it would make for grim reading. There would be uproar, and rightly so.

BELOW Richard Cockerill, Leicester's director of rugby, has had his run-ins with rugby's disciplinary authorities, including serving a four-week match-day ban in late 2009 for abuse of match officials.

There is always a line to be drawn. And for the most part, coaches know where it is. We need to cut them some slack. No matter that there might be the occasional blemish; the game is not off to hell in a handcart.

INTERNATIONAL SCENE

Sonny Bill Williams
Making the Switch

by RAECHELLE INMAN

'New Zealand coach Graham Henry was so taken with Williams' potential he broke with convention and courted him; the proud All Blacks are not in the habit of luring players home'

Never has there been a more dramatic defection from rugby league to rugby union. In 2008 Sonny Bill Williams was only 18 months into a five-year contract with Australian National Rugby League (NRL) club the Canterbury Bulldogs when he walked out. To make matters worse, his club was not notified of his defection until after Williams left for Europe. In an aftermath of massive controversy and numerous headlines, the matter was taken to the NSW Supreme Court and Williams was served with an injunction. It is understood his new French club Toulon paid a transfer fee of around £300,000 to the Bulldogs. At that time Williams was widely considered one of the most talented players in the NRL competition.

When Williams' contract with Toulon ended in June 2010, he again caused a massive stir. This time he rejected the largest offer to any player in rugby's history, a three-year deal with Toulon worth reportedly just under £4 million. New Zealand coach Graham Henry was so taken with Williams' potential he broke with convention and courted him; the proud All Blacks are not in the habit of luring players home. With the 2011 Rugby World Cup looming, Williams turned his back on the sizeable deal from Toulon to follow his dream of playing for the All Blacks in his native New Zealand. It is understood that by comparison the New Zealand Rugby Union (NZRU) are only paying him around £360,000 per year.

Williams was born in Auckland, New Zealand, and grew up playing rugby league. He was spotted by an Australian NRL talent scout and moved to Sydney at 16 years of age to play in the Bulldogs' junior grades and started in their Jersey Flegg Cup side in his first year.

In 2004, when he was only 18 years old, he made his NRL debut. It was a highly successful rookie season for Williams, who tasted Premiership triumph, coming off the bench in the Bulldogs' 16-13 victory over the Sydney Roosters in the grand final. That same year he was also named the 'International Newcomer of the Year' and debuted in the New Zealand national rugby league team against Australia in the ANZAC Test. Williams was consistently a top performer in league before switching codes. 'The biggest challenge [in my transition from league to union] was to confront my fear and be able to play at the highest level,' he confided. All Blacks coach Henry didn't waste any time, selecting Williams at centre for his country against England on 6 November 2010 at Twickenham. In his second game for the All Blacks, against Scotland, he impressively earned the man-of-the-match award.

In his quest to fulfil his dream of playing in the World Cup on home soil, Williams made a clever decision to sign with the Canterbury Crusaders in the Super Rugby competition. This has allowed him to build a strong partnership with All Blacks fly half Daniel Carter.

Crusaders coach and former All Blacks captain Todd Blackadder says Williams' first season in Super Rugby has been remarkable. 'When it comes to understanding the game, he is absolutely unbelievable how quickly he can learn,' Blackadder said.

FACING PAGE Sleight of hand. Sonny Bill Williams offloads the ball during a New Zealand training session ahead of the Test against England on 6 November 2010, Williams' All Blacks debut.

ABOVE Williams puts those offloading skills into practice during his man-of-the-match performance against Scotland on 13 November 2010.

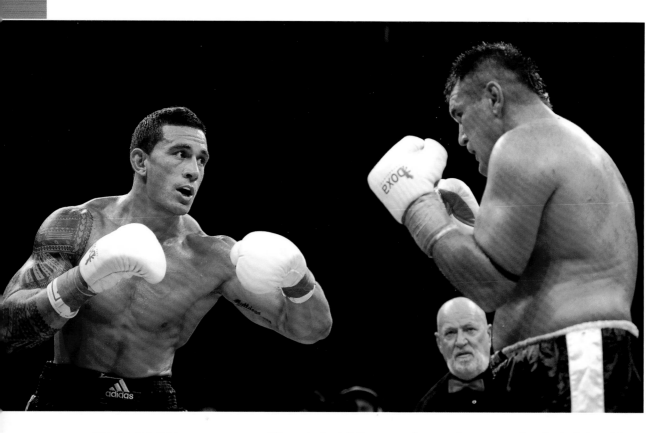

ABOVE All-round athlete. Williams takes on Australia's Scott Lewis on the Gold Coast in his third heavyweight bout, which he won on points. The New Zealander donated 200 tickets for the fight to Queensland flood victims.

FACING PAGE Sonny Bill runs at Jaque Fourie (No. 13) and Nick Koster as the Crusaders beat the Stormers 29-10 in Cape Town to advance to the 2011 Super Rugby final.

'If you look at it from purely a rugby perspective, he is doing things in his first year of Super Rugby that some of our guys can't do and they've played rugby all their lives,' he continued.

'He's the model professional. He's a gentleman. He's very intelligent. He's a real good down-to-earth humble guy. He works hard on his game. He is going to achieve.'

Williams sums up his introduction modestly: 'My first year in Super Rugby has been a learning experience and I continue to learn.'

'Representing the All Blacks means to me that I have been able to play for the ultimate rugby brand and if I am chosen to play in the World Cup that will be the pinnacle of my sporting career so far,' he continued. Williams clearly prizes playing at the elite level.

He is blessed with an explosive mix of athleticism, power, speed, size, skills and good football intuition; a dominant player with a unique ability to offload with finesse under pressure. Williams seems to have no real weakness. He is also a solid defender and a real team player; he is not selfish when it comes to scoring tries – an attribute the Crusaders and the All Blacks value.

'He could be one of the greatest players rugby has ever had,' Blackadder commented. 'Jonah Lomu was a great player, but he had limitations. Sonny, there's no limitations to how good this guy could be.

'He's a game-breaker and he has captured the imagination of the public, there's no doubt people go just to watch him.'

Williams certainly has the hopes of a nation resting on his broad shoulders. In 2010 he was the fifth most googled person in New Zealand.

While he is focused on achieving his ultimate goal of contributing to a Kiwi victory in the 2011 Rugby World Cup, he is also a heavyweight boxer; the only athlete to simultaneously pursue careers in both professional boxing and rugby. He says: 'Balancing two sports at once is extremely difficult, but as I gain more experience I will adapt better.'

He made his professional boxing debut in May 2009 and has won four from four. Williams negotiated in his agreement with the NZRU to be allowed three boxing bouts at agreed times during the rugby season. His latest two fights in 2011 have had a charity element to them, Williams doing his bit to help victims of natural disasters.

His third professional match, against Australian Scott Lewis, was moved from Australia's Newcastle to the Gold Coast to cross-promote the Crusaders' pre-season trial against the Queensland Reds. Williams donated 200 tickets to the Queensland flood victims. He then used the Crusaders' round 16 bye to fight Tongan Alipate Liava'a in Waitakere City, New Zealand. The match-up was dubbed 'The Clash For Canterbury' and became one of the single biggest fundraisers for the 2011 Christchurch earthquake appeal. Williams generously made a £50,000 donation from his share of TV sales – one of the biggest individual donations by an athlete to a disaster appeal.

Williams was in Christchurch when both the 2010 and 2011 Canterbury earthquakes struck. 'The earthquake rendered the building I was living in as unliveable. I am constantly reminded of it. The streets and landscape are no longer the same,' he said.

After a string of controversial off-field incidents whilst playing rugby league, Williams has changed his ways. He became a Muslim in 2008, gave up alcohol and now has a simpler life. Williams sums it up: 'I would describe myself as someone who is trying to better themselves as a person and as a sportsman.'

He has signed with the NZRU only until the end of the 2011 Rugby World Cup. At that stage he will evaluate his options and offers and may return to rugby league. Williams' future is the source of much speculation. One thing is certain: the code that secures him will benefit from showcasing a player with such devastating impact.

Finding solutions for the health and education sectors

Bucharest Rendezvous
the 2011 IRB Nations Cup

by CHRIS THAU

'Another coach who tested his credentials in the Nations Cup before taking over at the highest level is Springbok coach Peter de Villiers'

The return to Romania of the prestigious IRB Nations Cup tournament for the fifth consecutive year last June confirmed not only that the Romanian Rugby Federation had done a good job in managing and organizing the event but also that the participating teams were indeed happy in the environment provided by their hosts. 'The hotel was top quality, the food was excellent, the facilities absolutely wonderful. The tournament was well managed and the players enjoyed the experience,' enthused Portugal manager Rodrigo Santos Alves. It was the South African Kings who won the exciting tournament, with Georgia runners-up and the Argentina Jaguars in bronze-medal position. It was the third time the South African representatives had won the six-nation competition.

ABOVE Romania prop Mihaita Lazar bulldozes his way forward against Namibia. The IRB Nations Cup hosts won this opening match 13-11.

The Nations Cup started in Lisbon in 2006, with four competing teams – two Tier One nations sent sides (Italy A and Argentina A) and Russia and Portugal took part from Tier Three. The following year the tournament expanded to six nations and moved to Bucharest; it featured three Tier One teams (Italy A, Argentina A and Emerging Springboks) and three Tier Two nations (Romania, Georgia and Namibia). The Emerging Springboks, coached by Peter de Villiers, defeated Argentina A to win this second tournament; they returned the following year, with Chester Williams as head coach, to repeat their winning performance, this time playing hosts Romania in the final. In 2009, Scotland A had the better of France A in an exciting final that is still talked of in Bucharest; last year it was Namibia who surprised the pundits and perhaps themselves with their fine winning performance.

BELOW IRB tournament operations manager Beth Coalter with the Nations Cup and the captains of the six competing teams. From left to right: Ilia Zedginidze (Georgia), Mzwandile Stick (SA Kings), Jacques Nieuwenhuis (Namibia), João Goncalves Correia (Portugal), Marius Tincu (Romania) and Santiago Gonzáles Iglesias (Jaguars).

'The new format of the tournament, with six teams playing nine matches over a period of two weeks, was an outstanding success in every respect: it provided the participating teams with a positive experience in a tournament framework, had a big impact on the domestic Romanian scene providing a huge exposure for the game and has enabled a lot of players to experience the tournament environment and pressure. This is why we maintained both the venue and the format. Furthermore, the Nations Cup does not operate in isolation. It is part of a developmental blueprint which is aimed at increasing the overall competitiveness at Test level and Rugby World Cup of Tier Two and Three unions,' explained IRB tournament operations manager Beth Coalter.

The concept of a Nations Cup is not new. The IRB has launched in the past, within a different context and format, a tournament called the IRB Superpowers Cup – the brainchild of the late Vernon Pugh, the innovative IRB chairman who died eight years ago. Pugh understood quite early on that the current structure of the international game, overwhelmingly dominated by the Foundation Unions (the original eight members of the old IRFB), does not allow the emerging nations to stake their claim; he advocated the implementation of a programme that would lead to the addition of at least six other unions of similar playing standard and capability, increasing therefore the credibility and drawing power of RWC.

The original Superpowers Cup, involving the USA, Russia, Japan and China, failed to materialise due to the outbreak of the SARS epidemic in Asia in 2002. The following year the tournament, renamed the IRB Super Cup, was held in Tokyo, with Canada replacing China, who were not yet ready for this level of competition. Japan won the first tournament, and a second was pencilled in as the IRB launched its strategic plan designed to speed up the development of Tier Two countries into forces to be reckoned with on the international stage. The second IRB Super Cup, this time involving Japan, the USA, Canada and Romania and held in Tokyo in 2005, was equally successful and led to an expansion of the Nations Cup concept. The following year the first IRB Nations Cup was held in Portugal and further regional tournaments were launched elsewhere in the world.

'This is the way ahead. The Super Cup was definitely a success and some of the nations involved at the time have been keen to resurrect the concept. The International Rugby Board is looking into a more co-ordinated Tier Two and Tier Three Test programme; in other words, enable these nations to play each other more often, with different opponents, contexts and formats. The value of this approach has been amply demonstrated and we wish to diversify the way the Tier Two and Three nations play each other. That means we would like to facilitate bilateral and multilateral exchanges and obviously tours and this is something the IRB will look at in the future,' said Mark Egan, who is head of IRB High Performance and Development.

'We must give credit to Romania who have organised an outstanding tournament of genuine quality. The Nations Cup is not only great value for money, but also a positive event for the participants, Tier Two and Three unions who experience the inner workings and the routines of a tournament of this magnitude. Finally and equally significantly, the TV exposure of the event has grown exponentially as more and more nations buy the signal,' he added.

In addition to administrators and players, it is coaches and referees who have sharpened up their act in the boiling cauldron of the Arcul de Triumf national stadium in Bucharest during the last few years. On the Romanian side, former IRB development manager for Europe Robert Antonin has assembled a useful team of coaching talent, with former Romania centre Romeo Gontineac and former All Blacks prop Steve McDowall as the main men. Daniel Hourcade is the new coach of Argentina Jaguars, but two years ago their coaching team included former Pumas team-mates and friends Santiago Phelan and José Orengo. During the late 1990s and early 2000s, Phelan, who won 49 caps for the Pumas, was one of the mainstays of the Argentine back row; Orengo, meanwhile, a strong, hard-tackling centre, appeared 36 times for Argentina. They both finished their international

Sponsors of
Southern Hemisphere
rugby on Sky Sports

LEFT Romain Poite referees Argentina A v Italy A in the 2007 Nations Cup. At that time, Poite was an up-and-coming referee; he has now taken charge of high-profile Tests, including England v New Zealand in November 2010 and the 2011 Calcutta Cup match, during which he was forced off with a calf injury.

careers after RWC 2003, and now they coach the Pumas. The key to success in the words of Phelan is 'empowering the players'. 'We give them the tools, and it is up to them to choose what they do and how they do it. We do not believe in a straitjacket game. We preach a free-thinking game based on the players' intelligence and capacity to adapt,' Phelan said.

Another coach who tested his credentials in the Nations Cup before taking over at the highest level is Springbok coach Peter de Villiers, a former coach of South Africa Under 19 and Under 21, the latter world championship gold medallists in 2005. A former teacher, he believes that his job with the Emerging Springboks involved both coaching and mentoring. Like his Pumas counterparts, he wants his players to play 'the situation developing in front of them', and abhors patterns and structures. 'I don't want a game played by robots. I want creative talent at work, responding to challenges within a team framework,' he stated.

When Scotland A arrived in Bucharest two years ago, Andy Robinson had just been appointed the new Scotland coach. The performance of the team in Bucharest not only won Scotland their first ever gold medals in an IRB tournament but also strengthened the credibility of Robinson and his assistant Gregor Townsend, as well as relaunching the international career of their charismatic captain and scrum half Chris Cusiter. Mind you, the winning performance in 2010 of Namibia, with the firebrand flanker Jacques Burger as captain, also enhanced the status and credentials of their new coach Johan Diergaardt. The success this year of the South African Kings has confirmed not only the potential of the new South African franchise but also the excellence of their new coach Alan Solomons.

On the refereeing side the tournament has acted as a high-performance programme, as former tournament referees manager David McHugh observed. 'The Nations Cup has been doing wonders for newcomers to the international level. The international careers of several highly rated officials of the likes of Romain Poite of France, Peter Fitzgibbon of Ireland, Carlo Damasco of Italy, John Lacey of Ireland, England's JP Doyle were launched here in Bucharest. We also had Francisco Pastrana of Argentina and France's Jérôme Garcès, who was selected as an assistant referee for the World Cup, while last year we had here a mixture of very experienced referees of the likes of Marius Jonker of SA and up-and-coming talent of the likes of Aruna Ranaweera of USA, Canada's Bryan Arciero, SRU's Neil Paterson, James Jones of WRU.'

This year, in addition to Garcès, who returned to Bucharest for a second tour of duty before the World Cup, the tournament officials included two other high-flyers, 34-year-old French referee Pascal Gaüzère and 37-year-old Andrew Small of the RFU. The three referees were supported by a team of assistant referees which included two experienced Romanian officials in Horatiu Bargaunas and Vlad Iordachescu, well regarded in FIRA-AER senior competitions; Spain's up-and-coming Iñigo Atorrasagasti, son of former Spanish Test referee Iñaki Atorrasagasti; and Canada's Andrew McMaster. 'Refereeing standards in tournaments of this size and significance are expectedly high,' observed IRB referees manager Paddy O'Brien during the competition.

Red Renaissance
Queensland's Rugby Revival

by RAECHELLE INMAN

'The once-proud state, who won the amateur Super 10 competitions in 1994 and 1995, had become the laughing stocks of Super Rugby'

O n 9 July 2011, the Queensland Reds won the Super 15 final, beating the Canterbury Crusaders 18-13 in a thrilling encounter: a cycle in rugby was complete. The game was intense and fast-paced; it could have been a Test match. The Reds proved that they have the talent and resilience to compete with the best provincial sides in the world. Most of all it showed how far Queensland rugby has come. After years as perennial underperformers, they now have the mettle needed to win critical contests under pressure. In that match Reds half back Will Genia was outstanding, inspiring victory over the seven-time champions from Christchurch in front of a thunderous home crowd.

The significance of this game cannot be understated. The once-proud state, who won the amateur Super 10 competitions in 1994 and 1995, had become the laughing stocks of Super Rugby. They had not won a title since the game turned professional after the 1995 Rugby World Cup and consistently disappointed fans year after year.

Current Reds coach Ewen McKenzie explained. 'In the decade of the '90s Queensland had a lot of the best players in the world, such as John Eales, Tim Horan and Jason Little ... they had a good team and a good system and they were very consistent year in and year out and that went on for nearly a decade but things come to an end ... there are always cycles in sport. Around 2000 there was a change in coaching and some of those key individuals who had won a couple of World Cups retired ... it's a challenge for any sporting organisation when you lose key players as to what is sitting underneath and it is hard to hold talent when young players have world-class players in front of them. Some of those younger guys who would normally step up went elsewhere looking for opportunities and then when those champion players retired there was a void.'

'Queensland has won the national schoolboy title the last five years in a row so that tells you that there have been some good young players coming through, but there is competition in the marketplace and some of those players were syphoned off, such as David Pocock and James

RIGHT Queensland Reds fly half Quade Cooper lines up a kick at goal during the 2011 Super Rugby grand final at Brisbane's Suncorp Stadium. Cooper kicked two penalties and converted Digby Ioane's second-half try in his side's 18-13 victory. It was the Reds' first Super Rugby title since they beat Transvaal 30-16 in 1995 to win their second successive Super 10.

O'Connor, and they are really good players, so losing talent was still a problem mid-2000. We are working very hard at the moment to stop that flow,' he continued.

'The interesting thing about the schoolboy success is that those kids know how to win. They come out of school and they have played in successful campaigns and that is important as it is a mindset, it creates good habits.'

When McKenzie, a former Wallaby prop, took over as the Reds coach in 2010, the side could not win back-to-back games. He enjoyed immediate success in his first season, guiding the team to fifth place, their best result since 2002.

'You have to recognise it and do a lot of analysis about why you're losing .... When I started there last year our focus was just to win two games in a row and little things went into the process to achieve that goal. Sometimes we played more conservative football than we wanted to and sometimes we had to really push the envelope and tactically we have had to change the game every week. We didn't do the same thing so we had a lot of variety in there and that made more sense to generation Y, people who like change and not doing the same old thing each week,' he said.

McKenzie believes having a young, open-minded side and communicating effectively with the players puts them in a strong position. 'We have a great mindset in the playing group; they are up for change and new ideas which makes a massive difference,' McKenzie commented.

'If you look at the ages of most of the guys we are still one of the youngest teams in the comp. You go right through the team; we have James Slipper, Ben Daley and James Hanson in the front row and in the second row James Horwill and Rob Simmons, who has another ten years in the game. The back row is the same with Scott Higginbotham and Beau Robinson. Then in the backs we have Will Genia, Quade Cooper, Rod Davies and Luke Morahan. Most of them are 22 or 23 years of age so there's no reason they can't be around for a while.'

This strong pipeline is also a positive story for Australian rugby; many of these players will feature for the Wallabies in the 2011 Rugby World Cup in New Zealand and will also go on to the 2015 tournament in England.

Despite the inevitable injuries, the core Queensland side performs consistently from week to week, but having two young stars in the halves is obviously a great asset for the team. The retention of fly half Quade Cooper and 2011 Super 15 Player of the Year Genia cannot be underestimated in the Reds' quest for current and future success.

When he is at his best, New Zealand-born Cooper is brilliant in attack; he has great hands, a deceptive step and an impressive turn of pace. He hits the line flat and the defence cannot give him any leeway. A versatile player, Cooper can play at No. 10 as well as inside centre or full back.

In 2007 he made his senior debut for the Reds in his first year out of school, a year later making his debut for the Wallabies on the northern spring tour, scoring a match-winning try against Italy. In 2010 he was voted Super 14 Player of the Year in Australian rugby.

McKenzie rates the highly skilled Cooper among the best players he's coached in a career that extends from the NSW Waratahs to Stade Français and takes in stints as assistant coach at the Brumbies and Wallabies. 'In my mind he's been a brilliant No. 10,' he said.

'He's got that X-factor, but I think he's developed a balance in his game … I've coached plenty of players over the years and he's got one of the best packages I've been involved with in terms of communication, skill, understanding, game awareness and [he] puts in the background work as well.'

Cooper's creativity, organisation and combination with the in-form Genia has seen the Reds play to their potential this season. McKenzie uses his 9-10 combination to his side's advantage. The coach talks about 'creating reform' on their journey.

'We are a competitive team now. After last year a lot of people said when we finished fifth that we would struggle this year with "second year syndrome", especially with a young team, but we have done better and that's a good sign. We don't want to be a one year team; we are in it for the long haul, so we need to be building on the work. We built on last year and we will build again next year. You can't set your business up on winning titles every year, it is rare for a team in any sport to keep winning, so you set yourself up to be competitive and give yourself a chance to win and I think we've been doing that.'

Queensland rugby had to change its thinking and become more professional in order to become more competitive; choosing a coach with links to New South Wales and Victoria rather than the Sunshine State was crucial. 'There were a bunch of people who didn't want a non-Queenslander coaching the team … but I went there as a professional coach to do a job, they had been down for seven or eight years, they had a lot of false dawns and five or six coaches in that time. I knew I could change the things that needed changing, but I still had to do it.'

McKenzie says he used Queensland's parochial nature as an asset, investing in home-grown players and staff. This strategy coupled with the team's growing confidence has been winning back the fans.

After the Reds' one-point win over the Crusaders in their week 15 Super 15 clash on 29 May, hooker Saia Faingaa said the Reds believe they are invincible at rugby league's 'cauldron' Suncorp Stadium (formerly known as Lang Park). 'It feels like our fortress now and it feels like we can't lose there,' Faingaa said.

McKenzie agreed. 'The fan base is very connected now. They weren't in the past because they had a lot of disappointment … they are very enthusiastic now and you really notice when you play at home how engaged the fans are. The team really enjoys playing at home, it makes a big difference and it is probably helping us to get through in the tight games.'

The Reds boasted two Australian-record Super Rugby crowds of more than 48,000 and over 52,000 in their two home games against the Crusaders, and this support played a major role in their success, particularly in

CB RICHARD ELLIS

We are delighted to support the Wooden Spoon.

the Super 15 final. This new-found popularity is not just a boost for the team but also for the code in a competitive Australian football market.

The Reds' renaissance has seen the team double its home-game television audience in two years. They have become the most-watched Australian rugby union franchise on Australian television this season, a major achievement, given that there are many more subscribers in NSW than Queensland for Fox Sports. 'Our objective isn't to steal rugby league fans … the trick is to get people to turn up and watch. Watching on TV is one thing, but turning up to the games is the engagement we want, where they feel like they are part of the effort and the game against the Crusaders was the benchmark,' McKenzie said.

McKenzie is happy with the team's ethos. On field they are committed to supporting the ball carrier, a sign of a close-knit group. 'Everything you do has an impact on the team culture … if you assume the end goal you will come up short, you have to identify it, make sure everyone understands it, then make sure you live it and living it is the bit everyone struggles with.

'A million things have to come together but you have to be working and understanding that those million things are important … man management is the key, especially understanding the personalities … it can change pretty quickly, I don't get too depressed or too excited. If you watch me on the sideline you wouldn't know if we were winning or losing, I try to keep it pretty even.'

McKenzie is aware that depth of talent is the key to turning the current winning streak into long-term success to ensure sustainable achievement for the future. 'There is always change, while Queensland has its objectives, each person has their own objectives. The better you go the more attractive your players are elsewhere. We will be financially responsible. The trick from a coaching point of view is to always have the next individuals coming through, so you're not at the mercy of anyone, you can bring the next guy on so the talent identification and engagement of the next rung is very important, so I spend a lot of time there to make sure they are developing. It is a cycle.'

And the Queensland Reds completed this cycle in 2011 with a fairy-tale ending, securing their first Super Rugby title of the professional era.

BELOW Will Genia pins back his ears and heads for the line to score the winning try against the Crusaders.

PAGES 42-43 The magic moment. The Reds are Super Rugby champions once more.

You don't have to worry with us on your side

Car insurance with exceptional cover – 5 Star Defaqto Rated

defaqto
2011
★★★★★
CAR INSURANCE

Call our UK-only call centres on
0800 232 1474
For textphone first dial 18001.
Mon-Fri 8am-9pm, Sat 8am–5pm, Sun 9am-5pm. Calls may be recorded.
LV.com

LV= is proud to support Wooden Spoon

21121008 07/11

If you love it, LV♥= it

Blacks Almost Caught
the 2011 Junior World Championship
by ALAN LORIMER

'What was significant about England's challenge was their style of play. Gone was the bulldozer approach which has attracted criticism in the past'

If you thought that the Junior World Championship was becoming a series of exhibition matches for New Zealand rugby, then you might not be far off the mark. The 2011 tournament, staged in Padova (Padua), Treviso and Rovigo, was yet again won by New Zealand, who emphasised their domination of this tournament since its inception in 2008 with a fourth successive title.

ABOVE New Zealand's Baby Blacks celebrate winning the Junior World Championship for the fourth time in succession.

Fortunately for those looking for a different outcome, the apparent invincibility of the Baby Blacks was challenged by an England side that came close to upsetting New Zealand's 100 per cent record with a performance in the final that suggested a massive narrowing of the gap that has existed between the two countries in previous competitions.

New Zealand, winners over Australia by 62-17 in the 2010 championship final, were brought to heel in the 2011 final by an England side that arguably played the better attacking rugby but which was punished for errors in critical areas of the field. England, though, can take credit for matching New Zealand in the try tally, but in the end the men in white were beaten by the prodigious goal-kicking of New Zealand fly half Gareth Anscombe, who contributed 18 points with his unerringly accurate boot.

What was significant about England's challenge was their style of play. Gone was the bulldozer approach which has attracted criticism in the past, to be replaced by a fast, running game based on slick handling (from all 15) and clever moves orchestrated by fly half George Ford, a player surely destined to win senior honours in the very near future. A Leicester Tiger, Ford will not be the only graduate from this exceptionally gifted England side. Wasps wing Christian Wade showed

BELOW Christian Wade evades New Zealand full back Beauden Barrett during the final. Wade scored twice in the match to finish as joint top try scorer for the tournament with seven.

FACING PAGE Matt Lucas passes during the third-place play-off against France. The scrum half got on the scoresheet with a try in Australia's 30-17 win.

what a dangerous runner he is with two tries, while in the pack Charlie Matthews at lock and Alex Gray at No. 8 look set to win further honours. In the New Zealand side, meanwhile, flanker Sam Cane and fellow back-rower Luke Whitelock in the forwards and full back Beauden Barrett, showing the skills that made Christian Cullen such an exciting player, look set for career advancement.

New Zealand's place in the final was never in doubt after the Baby Blacks had crushed their opponents in the pool matches. Hosts Italy were the first to be put to the sword, before Wales suffered a 92-0 defeat, undoubtedly the major shock of the championship and one that triggered an immediate inquiry within Welsh rugby. New Zealand then cruised past Argentina to claim maximum pool points. England, by contrast, were made to work much harder in their pool, with a tough opener against Ireland and then an equally difficult game against Scotland, who surprised their southern neighbours by staying in contact until they gave away two soft scores in the final few minutes. In their final pool match England were pushed all the way but just had the measure of South Africa to win 26-20.

The Baby Boks, nevertheless, gained a bonus point from their defeat and looked to be in the frame for a semi-final place, only to be edged out by Australia. The latter side lost to France in the deciding game of Pool B, but also secured a bonus point to end up with a superior points difference, thus squeezing the Baby Boks out of the top four ranked countries.

Australia's higher points difference was very much down to a 54-7 win over a weakened Tonga side which had the frustration of having to do without 11 top players: four of them were in the New Zealand squad, four in the young Wallaby group, two selected by Fiji and one in the England team. South Africa, by contrast, had to battle hard against stiffer opposition in the form of both Ireland and Scotland for their pool points. But that is the luck of the draw and for this tournament it did not favour South Africa.

New Zealand then played Australia in the semi-finals, winning 37-7, while England achieved a repeat of their Under 20 Six Nations win over France, this time with a 33-18 scoreline. Australia looked the more likely bronze medallists, and in the event that was confirmed with a 30-17 Wallaby victory over France in the third-place play-off in Padova.

South Africa's frustration at missing out on a top-four finish was fully vented as the Baby Boks made sure that their second meeting with Ireland, in the fifth-place semi-final, resulted in a decisive win (57-15), then produced the highest score of the tournament in their 104-17 defeat of Fiji to finish in overall fifth place.

Fiji's collapse in the fifth-place play-off was as much a shock to the championship as it was to the islanders themselves. The Fijians had given France a fright in the pool matches and then had defeated Wales in the fifth-place semis. But against South Africa they had no answer to the Baby Boks' structured game – both in attack and defence – and powerful forward play. Still, a sixth-place finish for Fiji represents a massive advance for the Melanesians.

Wales, meanwhile, recovered sufficiently to defeat Ireland in the seventh-place play-off in a match between two demoralised sides. Argentina finished ninth after a close play-off match against Scotland that resulted in a 15-14 win for the young Pumas. In the relegation match Italy avoided the drop after defeating Tonga 34-22 at Rovigo to end up eleventh.

Results matter, but perhaps not as much as player development, in which context a rich seam of talent emerged. In the third-place play-off Australian scrum half Matt Lucas looked like a Wallaby in waiting, while for France, full back Geoffrey Palis caught the eye.

South Africa can expect much in the future from lock Eben Etzebeth, No. 8 Arno Botha, fly half Johan Goosen and centre Francois Venter. For Wales Matthew Morgan is another hugely talented player off the Welsh fly-half production line, and look out for lock Macauley Cook. Ireland have a number of promising players, among them prolific try scorer Andrew Conway, fly halves Paddy Jackson and James McKinney and lock Iain Henderson.

From the southern hemisphere island teams, Fiji centre Semi Radradra and Tonga back-rower Sam Finau impressed, while for Scotland threequarters Mark Bennett and Kerr Gossman and scrum half Sean Kennedy registered strong performances. Argentina, traditionally strong in age-grade rugby, were disappointed with their ninth-place finish, but they can take satisfaction from the play of their fly half Sebastián Poet and the collective strength of their pack. Power up front was Italy's hallmark, and it would be surprising if their front row of Nicola Quaglio, Andrea Lupetti and

RIGHT Semi Radradra of Fiji tackles Arno Botha in the Baby Boks' 104-17 demolition of the islanders in the fifth-place play-off. No. 8 Botha scored a hat-trick in the match to leave him level with England's Christian Wade on seven tries for the tournament.

FACING PAGE Lock Iain Henderson has his pursuers labouring in his wake during Ireland's 30-13 win over Scotland in Pool C.

Piermaria Leso were not to appear in the senior team within the next few years. Another to keep track of in the Italy side is scrum half Guglielmo Palazzani.

The championship was not without its off-field interest. Midway through the tournament, a story broke in the Irish press that Ireland were pulling out of next year's competition because of 'player welfare concerns'. At the time of the tournament, both the IRFU and the IRB refused to confirm or deny the story, but sources close to the Irish authorities claimed it was a done deal and that moreover Scotland and Wales were considering their positions. The Irish had reportedly voiced concerns about the pressure that five games in 17 days put on young players. A fair point, of course, and one that might be answered by either lengthening the time span of the tournament or increasing the size of squads from 26 to 35 (say), or both. Unions must weigh the developmental benefits that accrue from participating in a global tournament (and hence playing the best sides in the world) against the demands put on young players, many of whom are putting at risk their university studies.

While the 2011 Junior World Championship in Italy was generally accepted as a success, there were questions raised about the scheduling of matches on finals day. Whereas the third-place play-off and final began in Padova at 1700 and 1910 respectively, the four matches to decide places five to 11, divided between Treviso and Rovigo, kicked off at 1200 and 1410 in temperatures of up to 32 degrees Celsius. If that did not raise concerns about player welfare, then it should have. It was simply lunacy to play rugby in those conditions and it should have been avoided.

Next year, when the tournament is hosted by South Africa in Cape Town and Stellenbosch, high temperatures should not be an issue, but what still may be contentious is the compressed time span of the tournament and the issue of squad sizes. The world championship at Under 20 level is in so many ways an admirable tournament, but if it is to retain universal support its format may have to be re-examined. That is a matter for the IRB. Meanwhile, after a tournament of sunny rugby in sunny Italy, roll on South Africa.

Return of the Kings
the Cape's New Franchise

by CHRIS THAU

'Eastern Province has a long and glorious rugby tradition. The union was founded in 1888 and it was the first to host a Lions Test, at Port Elizabeth'

The South African Kings, who made their international debut at the IRB Nations Cup last summer, are a rugby franchise with a difference. Their real name is the Eastern Province Kings or Southern Kings, and they hail from one of the powerhouses of South African rugby, the Eastern Cape, with its two large unions, the Eastern Province Rugby Union (EPRU) and Border Rugby Football Union (BRFU), as the main shareholders. Their objective is to join Super Rugby (currently Super 15) by 2013, which, based on their first-year performances in domestic South African competitions under head coach Alan Solomons, could be described as perfectly feasible.

In the recent past, various attempts to harness the enormous potential of Eastern Cape rugby have failed for a variety of reasons. That was before the new president of the Eastern Province Rugby Union, Daniel 'Cheeky' Watson, set his mind to it. 'And when dad puts his mind onto

something, nothing in the world could stop him,' his son Luke, a Springbok and former Bath captain, said with a chuckle.

Playing Super Rugby for their own team is an attraction very few born-and-bred Port Elizabeth rugby men could resist, and Luke Watson has left the English Premiership to return home for the last and probably most significant experience of his playing career. He expects his homecoming, taking into account his vocal rejection of some of the sacred cows of South African rugby, to generate 'opposition, resistance and a lot of animosity'. Perhaps the firebrand youngster has mellowed, with the Bath interlude helping him to relax and re-evaluate his life and career in a more positive context.

There are many similarities between the articulate youngster and his charismatic father – one of the genuine heroes of the anti-apartheid struggle in South Africa. Both father and son have been precocious rugby talents and both are driven by their strong religious beliefs. Both

ABOVE The driving force behind the Kings project. Cheeky Watson (left), with son Luke who plays for the new franchise.

FACING PAGE Kings full back and captain Mzwandile Stick brings down Romania back-rower Ovidiu Tonita during the 2011 IRB Nations Cup in Bucharest. The South African side won the match 27-23.

are low-key, calm individuals, who although they despise confrontation will defy authority, adamantly standing their moral ground. Both believe that rugby is a way of life rather than a game and has to be played and lived accordingly – a moral dimension that brought them into conflict with the establishment of the game and in some cases with fellow players and coaches.

It is their religious beliefs that have been the main driving force in the lives of the Watsons (they are heirs to a Charismatic Evangelical tradition going back to the beginning of the 19th century) since their ancestors left Scotland to settle in the Cape Colony. Luke's grandfather Daniel John Watson was a farmer and a coach at the local rugby club, Crusaders, which was attended by his four sons, Gavin, Ronnie, Valance and Cheeky, of whom Valance and Cheeky became Eastern Province regulars. During the 1970s, apartheid was at its height, with the blacks confined to their own areas (townships) and the whites playing among themselves. Rugby was the elite game of the

establishment, and anybody daring to break the strict and repressive apartheid regulations was dealt with ruthlessly.

'I grew up in a very hostile environment, with scaring phone calls, police knocking down the door to get into the house, with father frequently arrested, but to be honest it did not affect me too much,' says Luke Watson. 'First I grew used to it and then you start to somewhat expect it. Then I was not really that aware of what my dad was standing for and doing, but I was lucky to have my mother Tracy alongside – she has been a mountain of strength throughout this ordeal – the family, friends and more significantly our beliefs that we are doing the right thing.

'But this endless fight took its toll, made me very defensive and quite confrontational as a person. What my father did was to fight for freedom and for a while I became an extension of that struggle. Now I have grown older and I would say wiser. The time at Bath has helped; a wonderful town with great rugby people. No more limelight, just the anonymity of being myself, playing and enjoying the game. It enabled me to take a good look at myself and decide for a new course of action. Now is time to look at my own legacy … write my own life story. Now my life is about reconciliation! This is why I decided to come back to Port Elizabeth, because I had an opportunity to make an impact, make a contribution for the better, no matter how small that might be. I have got married and have got a two months old girl. That has changed my life. I am probably mellowing, but I am not less resilient by any means.

'Cheeky wants this to be a success, which he believes will change the face of SA rugby. This team has the potential to bring a new dynamic and a new demography to SA rugby. I believe that if successful it will truly change the way things have been done in South Africa. It will create an incredible opportunity for the disadvantaged people in our area. We already have three to four guys from townships in this team, some of whom went out of South Africa [to the IRB Nations Cup in Bucharest] for the first time in their lives. This speaks volumes about what dad is trying to create.'

Another one to head home to join the newly born franchise is head coach and director of rugby Solomons, born in Uitenhage in the Eastern Cape in 1950 and until last year an IRB High Performance consultant. 'For me this is a homecoming. These are my roots, and it is quite exciting and privileged to be part of this project that would leave such a legacy. The Eastern Cape and the Border region is the cradle of black rugby in South Africa and in years gone by, in the apartheid era, the blacks were not given an opportunity. Now that democracy has come to SA they are given equal opportunities, and what you find is that there are fantastic black players coming out of our schools, and this is something you can see in our academy. Because the bulk of our population is black, I believe that in the times to come, this side will represent the demographics of the country.'

Solomons, a former captain and coach of Cape Town University under Cecil Moss, whom he describes as his mentor, has got a tremendous coaching background which includes the Western Province, the Western Stormers, Northampton and Ulster, as well as South Africa and the Barbarians as an assistant coach to Nick Mallett. He has got a deep understanding of the Eastern Cape and its rugby tradition. Joining the Kings as head coach and director of rugby was a sign of his confidence in both the project and the man who drives it forward – Cheeky Watson, the Eastern Province Rugby Union president. 'Cheeky is absolutely critical to this franchise. He is the key man and is brilliant to work with and the CEO Anele Pamba. When I was young I did not know him personally but had seen him playing and he was absolutely outstanding. I knew one of his brothers Ronnie, with whom I went to Grey School,' Solomons said.

'Two years ago, all of a sudden I got a call from Cheeky asking whether I was prepared to coach the EP team against the British & Irish Lions. I said yes, having checked with Mark Egan whether I could take a couple weeks off my work with the IRB. We did not do too badly, though we lost 20-8. After the match Cheeky asked me whether I was prepared to take this job ... I said I would do it if we get a Super Rugby franchise. Then we realised that it was a chicken and the egg situation. On

The partners of

THE SR GROUP

are proud to sponsor and support the Wooden Spoon

We recruit across the legal, tax, marketing, support, search and HR sectors within the banking and financial services, professional services, commerce & industry and legal industries.

For all of your recruitment needs, please contact Nick Root on
+44 (0)20 7415 2828
or email him at
nickroot@taylorroot.com

the one hand SARFU was saying that we must improve the standard of rugby in the region before we could get a franchise while we were saying that unless we get a franchise nobody was going to come here to PE. So I said, "OK. Let's do it!" We started in June 2010 ... Last year we won division one and lost in the final ... This year we strengthened the squad, strengthened the coaching staff, the academy is up and running. The facilities at the Mandela Bay Stadium are absolutely first class. So we have made huge strides.'

This was an opportunity not to be missed for 27-year-old Kings captain and full back Mzwandile Stick, a former captain of the Springbok Sevens team whose dreadlocks and fierce tackling had become his trademarks on the IRB Sevens circuit. An outside half and full back at Newell HS, Stick reached the Eastern Province Under 16 age-group side, then made an impression for EP Under 18s in Craven Week two years later. The Sharks offered the youngster a professional contract in 2004, the year he made his debut for Paul Treu's Springbok Sevens team. The launch of the Eastern Province Kings has convinced the player to return to Port Elizabeth to revive his 15-a-side career and be part of 'the history the Kings will create'.

Eastern Province has a long and glorious rugby tradition. The union was founded in 1888 and it was the first to host a Lions Test, at Port Elizabeth: indeed that opening match of the 1891 inaugural Test series against the British team captained by Bill Maclagan was the birth of South Africa as a Test nation. For more than a century Port Elizabeth has been a vibrant rugby centre, with its various ethnic groups divided by the odious apartheid system, yet somehow united through a common passion for rugby.

The newly founded franchise was launched with a match against the British & Irish Lions in 2009, which was watched by almost 36,000 spectators. Eastern Cape is a rugby-hungry territory with a population of 16.5 million says the union marketing leaflet. In 2010 the EPRU requested permission to use the word 'Kings' at the Eastern Cape House of Traditional Leaders, out of respect for tradition and the kings of the Xhosa, the dominant ethnic group of the Eastern Cape. The blessing was granted. Their objective is quite ambitious: to become the biggest union in South African rugby within the next five years and perhaps more significantly to be truly representative of all inhabitants of South Africa and to showcase the Eastern Province talent in an international arena.

BELOW Kings in Romania. Skipper Mzwandile Stick holds aloft the IRB Nations Cup in Bucharest.

Short Game Pioneers
the 2011 Hong Kong Sevens
by IAN ROBERTSON

'In 30 years so much has changed, but also so much has stayed the same. The tournament has expanded, but still the minnows have the opportunity to take on the big fish'

It was hard to believe that the 2011 Hong Kong Sevens marked the thirtieth anniversary of my first visit in 1981. A lot has changed in the intervening period, although fortunately the tradition and ethos have remained constant.

My recollection of that first expedition in 1981 is a little hazy, but I do remember we had to break the journey in each direction in Bahrain and when we eventually reached Hong Kong the two key venues were the Furama Hotel and the Football Stadium. The Furama has long since gone and the success of the Sevens meant a new, much bigger venue was needed. Hence my two focal points became the wonderful Hilton Hotel and the magnificent Government Stadium. Sadly the Hilton is

also no more. Moreover, the Hong Kong Sevens no longer remain the only major Sevens event on the world map but have become part of the IRB's burgeoning Sevens circuit, now under the sponsorship of HSBC.

Without the 35 years of the Hong Kong Sevens, I wonder if we would have had glamorous venues such as Buenos Aires, Las Vegas and Dubai, which make up the HSBC Sevens World Series circuit today along with established rugby strongholds like New Zealand, Australia and South Africa. If it had not been for the Hong Kong Sevens, I wonder if Sevens rugby would be included in the 2016 Olympic Games in Rio de Janeiro. There is no doubt the Hong Kong Sevens were the pioneers, and Sevens becoming an Olympic sport is the ultimate recognition.

In 30 years so much has changed, but also so much has stayed the same. The tournament has expanded to include 24 countries, but still the minnows have the opportunity to take on the big fish. In 2011 Mexico were invited for the first time and were able to play against Scotland, Samoa and Tonga in the pool stages. Sadly the major International Board countries – New Zealand, Australia, South Africa, England, Scotland, Ireland, Wales and France – no longer send any of their established and famous 15-a-side players. The glorious days of David Campese, Andy Irvine, Jonah Lomu, Hugo Porta, Andy Ripley and dozens more household names appearing in Hong Kong are gone forever. That is disappointing but inevitable in the professional game. The good news is that the Sevens are still a massive sporting event in Hong Kong and a capacity crowd of over 40,000 witnessed yet another great extravaganza of all that is best in the abbreviated game.

As has always happened, the fledgling teams produced occasional brilliant performances to surprise rugby's giants. From 2011, my memories will be of Russia leading England, the eventual runners-up, by seven points to five with only 33 seconds of the match remaining (England eventually came through 10-7). That was a remarkable scoreline near the end of an amazing match,

ABOVE Russia's Alexander Yanyuskin hauls Mitieli Nacagilevu of Fiji out of play as the latter attempts to touch down during the pool stage in Hong Kong. Fiji won this encounter 29-14.

FACING PAGE Star of Afrika. Cecil Afrika dives over Joseph Gardener (name misspelled on shirt) to score for South Africa against Portugal in the semi-finals of the Plate.

"That degree won't get you anywhere."

Conservative uncle

33° N – Zanskar, India

Live life without boundaries

When your children finish school, they won't be short of well-meant advice. But whether you encourage them to trust their instincts or your experience, you'll want to be able to support their education financially. Speak to HSBC Premier about creating a plan for your children's education.

HSBC Premier is subject to financial eligibility criteria and is available in over 40 countries and territories.

www.hsbcpremier.com

HSBC **Premier**

HSBC

The world's local bank

and this was not in a pool game – this was in the Cup quarter-finals. The points scorers for Russia – Sergey Sugrobov (try) and Alexander Yanyuskin (conversion) – may well go on to greater things, and their inspiration will be the 2016 Olympics. Indeed in an earlier pool match, Russia only trailed Fiji 17-14 going in to the final minute.

And what about Portugal? They only lost to mighty New Zealand 19-12 in the pool stage, which was a fantastic achievement. Canada, like Portugal, had their moment of glory – or, as Andy Warhol would say, their 15 minutes of fame. They beat current world champions Wales 24-17 in the Bowl semi-finals. The Sevens remains a perfect stage for the smaller rugby nations to parade their skills. Thus it has ever been. Long may it continue.

The tournament is split into four competitions on the final day, which has been a big success and gives every team a chance of winning a prize at their own level. For the record, at the bottom end Kenya won the Shield, beating Spain 17-12, while in the Bowl final, Canada, after their success against Wales in the semis, beat Japan 33-12. South Africa had a well-deserved win over Australia by 26 points to 19 in the Plate final, with Cecil Afrika the Springbok star and a name to watch in the future.

The Cup went to the all-conquering New Zealand team. Having already won the top trophy in George in South Africa and Wellington in New Zealand, they notched up their third victory in the 2010-11 HSBC Sevens World Series by beating England 29-17, in the process winning the Cup for the tenth time in Hong Kong. Their win was a fitting end to three action-packed days of Sevens rugby.

BELOW Ben Gollings and James Rodwell of England pull down Bryce Heem in the Cup final. Gollings retired from international Sevens at the end of the 2010-11 season as the World Series career top scorer. He totalled 2652 points, more than twice as many as second-placed Waisale Serevi of Fiji.

PAGES 60-61 Hong Kong is but one stop in the HSBC Sevens World Series. The following pages give a flavour of the modern international Sevens game, on the road around the world from December to May.

1ST INNINGS
2ND INNINGS

CURRENT GAME

NEW ZEALAND   2 8

SOUTH AFRICA   2 0

Talbot Underwriting is proud
to support the Wooden Spoon Charity.

We continue our association with the In Touch programme
and recently became a sponsor of Spoon's new inspirational project,
Game On! a high profile programme to address prevalent social issues
with those young people not in employment, education or training.

TALBOT
VALIDUS GROUP

www.talbotuw.com

Saxons Succeed Again
the 2011 Churchill Cup

by HUGH GODWIN

'The Saxons have only two matches scheduled for 2012, and Lancaster admitted the end of the Churchill Cup might hurt England more than anyone'

The ninth and last Churchill Cup was won by England Saxons at Worcester's Sixways Stadium in mid-June. It was a predictable outcome, for though Canada put up a commendable fight in the final, their efforts combined with those of the USA, Russia and first-time participants Italy A and Tonga were short of the sustained quality or physical conditioning required to worry a team treated to the comforting benefit of playing the competition at home.

The demise of the 'buddy' arrangement between England, Canada and the USA that began with a three-team competition in Vancouver in 2003 was signalled in May 2010, when the International Rugby Board Council approved a new, global ten-year playing schedule to begin in 2012. This timetable featured a shift in emphasis from stand-alone competitions to two- or three-match Test series between Tier One unions, plus tours to the Pacific Islands, North America and Japan as part of an 'integrated Tier Two schedule'.

Eddie O'Sullivan, the former Ireland coach now guiding the US Eagles, expressed the uncertain hope that whatever itinerary replaced the Churchill Cup would be at least as focused and challenging for his side. For the time being, O'Sullivan said the only logical way forward was to follow the Argentina and Pacific Islander model of developing players abroad. 'Our tipping

RIGHT Patrick Danahy of the Eagles tussles with England Saxons' Dave Attwood to secure line-out ball at Franklin's Gardens. The Saxons overpowered the USA 87-8.

point is to get another five or six guys overseas in the next couple of years,' he said. But this is a double-edged sword. After a long European club season and with the Churchill Cup falling before the pre-World Cup player-release window, the USA did without Chris Wyles and Hayden Smith of Saracens as well as Mike MacDonald of Leeds, Takudzwa Ngwenya of Biarritz and Samu Manoa, the lock who has signed for Northampton.

In a now familiar format, two pools of three teams each were decided by a Saturday-Wednesday-Sunday series of double-headers at Northampton, Esher and Gloucester respectively. Then on to Worcester – the twentieth Churchill Cup match venue since 2003 – for the finals of Cup, Plate and Bowl. Under the coaching of Stuart Lancaster, Simon Hardy and Jon Callard – but not the captaincy of Luke Narraway, who pulled out injured before a ball was passed – the Saxons (as England's A team has been known since the 2006 Churchill Cup) captured their sixth title with comfortable victories over the USA (87-8) and Tonga (41-14) in Pool A before a 37-6 defeat of Canada in the final.

At the end of it, three Saxons were named in England's 45-man World Cup training squad. The call-up for the Saracens prop Matt Stevens was long anticipated. Gloucester wing Charlie Sharples and Saracens lock Mouritz Botha belonged more to the 'bolter' category. Overall the average age of

23 in the Saxons' final line-up indicated the greater importance was in developing players for the next one or two World Cup cycles, not the current one.

Deprived of their famous five, and with captain Todd Clever rested, the USA took a 13-try thrashing from the Saxons as the tournament kicked off on Northampton's carpetlike pitch. Miles Benjamin celebrated his club Worcester's recent promotion back to the Premiership with three tries and the other scorers included the Exeter flanker Tom Johnson, a new face at this level.

In Pool B, Italy A led 9-6 against Canada at half-time at Franklin's Gardens, before No. 8 Aaron Carpenter drove over from a five-metre scrum and prop Jason Marshall also scored from short range. James Pritchard took a perfect line in support of Chauncey O'Toole's break to claim Canada's third and final try after 56 minutes of a 26-12 win.

The following Wednesday, in that part of south London where the suburbs meet rural Surrey, the Esher club gave a proud welcome to the USA and their Tongan opponents. The match and the night belonged to Viliame Iongi, Tonga's left wing, who scored the first four of his side's five tries in a 44-13 win – a one-man bonus point, you might say. Iongi's last was his best: taking a pass on halfway as Tonga fielded a USA drop-out, he sprinted up the middle between two opponents and blazed round the Eagles' Colin Hawley with a knifing sidestep.

Coached by Kingsley Jones, the former Wales captain and Sale Sharks coach, Russia got their second Churchill Cup campaign under way against Canada in the second Esher fixture. Jones had rested five of his top players for the Churchill Cup. 'Russia have got a lot of creative players but we need to create a platform to give them some space,' Jones said, with a hint of trepidation. In the event, Canada's O'Toole was man of the match for the second time in five days and scored one of his side's five tries as they won Pool B with a 34-18 defeat of the Russians. 'It feels pretty good to be in the final – that was our goal,' said O'Toole, and the flanker would go on to be named the competition's 'most valuable player'.

There was rain and an unseasonal chill at Gloucester, but the Saxons warmed the cockles of every Kingsholmite's heart with an extraordinary three penalty tries from scrums against a bewildered Tonga. French referee Romain Poite punished the Pacific Islanders' loose-head props Tonga Lea'aetoa and Ofa Fainga'anuku (a replacement, who was shown a yellow card after the third penalty try in the 62nd minute) as well as tight-head and captain Kisi Pulu during an almighty skewering led by Stevens and loose-head Matt Mullan. Other England tries went to Jordan Crane – the stand-in captain for his positional rival Narraway – and his Leicester clubmate Billy Twelvetrees. Rory Clegg, the Harlequins fly half who played every minute of the Saxons' three matches, kicked five conversions and two penalties.

Russia, with 11 changes, continued in their watchable, uncomplicated style, but though they raised a Kingsholm roar with a length-of-the-field try for left wing Rushan Yagudin, they lost 24-19 to the Italians, who qualified for the Plate final. Gloucester old boy Marco Bortolami and new Kingsholm recruit Dario Chistolini were among those used from the bench.

In a clash of the USA and Russia that will be repeated at the World Cup, the Bowl was won by the Eagles, 32-25. Paul Emerick scored the opening try after 23 minutes when he found a gap after some ponderous rucks, but tries by Vladimir Ostroushko and Alexander Voytov had the Bears 18-11 up ten minutes into the second half. Then hefty Eagles centre Andrew Suniula stepped through the Russians to score, and captain Clever made a 60-metre interception to flip the seven-point advantage around. Though Vasily Artemyev, one of the stand-out players of the 2010 Churchill Cup, went over for Russia to make the score 25-25, a counterattack led by full back Blaine Scully led to the clinching try by replacement Tai Enosa from Suniula's pass.

Tonga had Tomasi Sili, a Catholic priest, at centre for the Plate final and the effervescent Iongi slipped a tackle for a lovely try in the 54th minute. But any possible 'wing and a prayer' headline never made it to the printed page. Emboldened by Riccardo Bocchino's early try, running against the grain off a steady scrum, Italy A prevailed 27-18.

Canada were wounded before the Cup final by losing the experienced Justin Mensah-Coker and Ed Fairhurst to work commitments, but Carpenter, of Plymouth Albion, made a record twentieth Churchill Cup appearance in his sixth tournament. The Saxons, with their scrum power assured, concentrated on applying pressure at the line out; Dave Attwood, a World Cup hopeful, was out injured, but the roving James Gaskell complemented Botha and the Leicester-bound Graham Kitchener nicely. Mimicking the style of Gloucester's backs, England set to work launching Sharples on narrow and wide angles from set-pieces, and if much of the play was far from watertight the Saxons' hallmark was an ability to tidy up loose ends.

Thus an unconvincing incursion by Sharples became a try for Gaskell in the right-hand corner after 21 minutes: 8-3. And a trundle and fumble by the English forwards after the restart became a 55-metre try for Benjamin when he intercepted Ciaran Hearn's pass: 15-3 with Clegg's conversion to add to his opening penalty. Ander Monro had dropped a goal for Canada, and the evergreen Pritchard kicked a penalty before half-time, but the Saxons pressed on. Clegg's high cross-kick made Benjamin's second try on 59 minutes, and Botha's speed onto scrum half Paul Hodgson's box kick set up Sharples' try with 13 minutes remaining. London Irish flanker Jamie Gibson rounded off another hurly-burly attack – Clegg was required to volley a fluffed pass before Trinder straightened the move – and Clegg converted to finish with 12 points.

The Saxons have only two matches – against Ireland A and Scotland A – scheduled for 2012, and Lancaster admitted the end of the Churchill Cup might hurt England more than anyone. 'We need to continue to create development opportunities,' he said, 'to bridge the gap between the Premiership and international rugby.' A moment, perhaps, to pluck a quote from the vast stock bequeathed by the prime minister and wartime leader whose name was taken by the now defunct competition. 'I am an optimist,' Winston Churchill once said. 'It does not seem too much use being anything else.'

FACING PAGE Dario Chistolini, on as a replacement, tries to halt Russia's fly half Yuri Kushnarev at Kingsholm, where the Italy A prop will turn out for Gloucester in 2011-12.

BELOW Icing on the cake. Jamie Gibson sets off for the line to score the Saxons' fifth try of the final against Canada.

"Wishing the Wooden Spoon every success with their ongoing work"

INSPIRING COMMUNITIES CHANGING LIVES

The Saracens Sport Foundation aims to inspire communities and change lives through the power of sport. Through the Saracens brand, professional players and high quality staff, we engage and challenge children and young people to lead an active, healthy and rewarding lifestyle.

To find out more about the work of the Saracens Sport Foundation and how you can support our work, visit www.saracens.com/foundation or call us on 01707 268 919

SARACENS SPORT FOUNDATION

HOME FRONT

The Rovers Return
London's Exiles Meet Again

by **CHRIS JONES**

'November's match is a welcome reminder of the 'old days' of London rugby, when a meeting between the exiles would grab the headlines'

Squeezing into a Richmond pub will be one of the toughest assignments any rugby supporter will attempt on 19 November this year. On that day, London Welsh will host London Scottish for the first time in the English Championship – the second division – in a hugely significant match that marks the return of the Scots to the upper levels of the English game.

Having been cast down nine divisions to the bottom rung of the RFU leagues when the club's professional arm went under in 1999, the Scots have fought their way back with seven promotions in 11 seasons to set up the long-awaited return to fully competitive clashes with their Welsh neighbours down the road.

The Scots were founded in 1878 at Mackay's Tavern in Ludgate Hill, while the Welsh came onto the scene in 1885. November's match is a welcome reminder of the 'old days' of London rugby, when a meeting between the exiles would grab the headlines and fill the coffers of local pubs and clubs as thousands of fans enjoyed a battle which featured British & Irish Lions stars in abundance.

Now, both clubs are very much part of the modern era of rugby in England, with the only difference being the financial commitment each is making to the new season. While the Welsh have found the financial clout to field a fully professional squad under new coach Lyn Jones, formerly at the Ospreys, the Scots, coached by Simon Amor, are semi-professional, training three times a week in the evenings, allowing their players to be employed elsewhere in the capital while still playing at the level just below the Premiership.

It's all about cutting your cloth, and even their off-the-field operations mirror a different attitude to Championship rugby and the potential to break into the top flight. Former Lions flanker John Taylor is the Welsh managing director and oversees a club that has had to overcome serious cash problems in recent years as it attempts to regain former glories

ABOVE Simon Amor of London Scottish spins the ball out to his backs against Esher in January 2010. Amor, a former England Sevens captain, is now the head coach at Scottish.

FACING PAGE John Taylor, today managing director at London Welsh, launches a kick at goal for the club against London Irish in 1972.

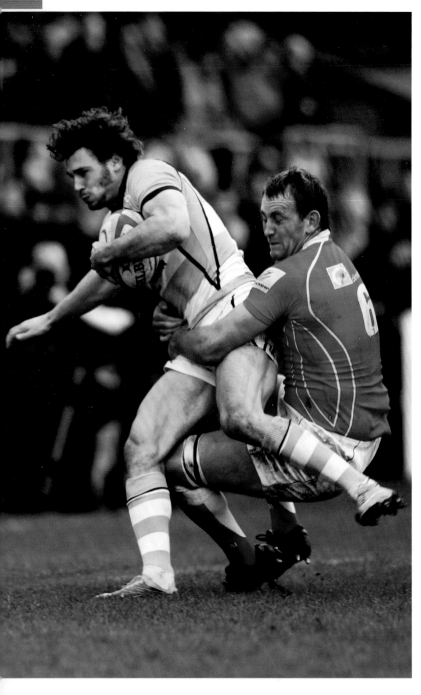

as one of the biggest names in club rugby. Tony Copsey is the part-time CEO of London Scottish, running his own consultancy company as well as helping the Scots prepare for life in the Championship.

Neither club would satisfy the stringent criteria for entry to the Premiership, and while the Welsh would put into operation plans to meet the stadia and other requirements, the Scots are happy to launch their next five-year growth plan and see where they stand at the end of that period. Consolidation is the aim for the Scots after their amazing promotion to the Championship through coming out on top in a winner-takes-all match at Barking on their final day of last season.

The Welsh, by contrast, were heavily involved in the controversial play-off system operated for clubs trying to earn the right to join the Premiership; they were beaten in the semi-finals by Cornish Pirates, prompting a change in emphasis in their squad for this season, with bigger forwards drafted in to deal with what Taylor describes as the 'lumpy' packs you have to arm-wrestle at this level of rugby. Like the Welsh, the Scots have new faces in key coaching positions, with Alex Codling, the former England lock, taking over the forwards, having previously been in charge at Barking.

Both exiles clubs have to operate under the new English Qualified Player (EQP) quotas in the Championship, which, patently, throws up particular problems for teams who are proud of their continuing strong links with 'home'.

Taylor, who will miss the opening two months of the season as he is Talksport's lead commentator at the Rugby World Cup in New Zealand, explained, 'Under the EQP we must have 14 English-qualified players in our match squad and at Welsh we have players who have played for Wales at Sevens and that does complicate matters because they cannot be counted as English even though they do satisfy the residential qualifications. That then limits the numbers of overseas players you can sign from places such as Fiji and Tonga.

'The Championship is very challenging financially because we don't get substantial support from the RFU and that is why we are aiming to get into the Premiership within the next two seasons. We have a number of backers and are funded for the season at a level to have a very competitive squad that is full-time. There are still a couple of shakedowns before professional rugby finally settles down in England and some clubs do not want to satisfy the criteria for promotion.

'The return of London Scottish is very positive because it revives a fantastic old rivalry and the market won't be damaged – in fact it will stimulate things.'

Copsey, who played a major role in creating the successful 'brands' at Harlequins, Saracens and London Wasps, said, 'The EQP criteria have to be managed and around 40 per cent of our squad is Scottish-qualified and we want that higher but a lot of them are dual-qualified – genuine London exiles who have lived down here for a long time. Longer-term the EQP may be an issue but it isn't at the moment.

'Like the Welsh, our heritage is massively important. We have some fully retained players but don't pay them full-time and we feel that's the best way forward without taking our wage bill north of £1 million. The major hurdle to promotion is the criteria and you have to accept that the Premiership is a different financial league with Quins a £13 million turnover business while we are turning over just over £1 million so it's a massive gulf. In my view, it's about improving within a five-year cycle and our short-term ambition is to become a sustainable Championship outfit – self-financing – then improving facilities in the future.

'This club has benefited massively from the commitment of the board who have all played for the club and have a 'feet-on-the-ground' approach and we all know that southwest London is a very competitive rugby market. However, we can carve out a niche market with so many Scottish exiles living in London. The comeback story of London Scottish is quite incredible and I am hugely excited to be part of this club.'

Sarries Make It Theirs
the 2010-11 Aviva Premiership
by CHRIS HEWETT

'To their enormous credit, Saracens carried on clinching for the rest of the campaign, losing a mere four games in total and none at all after the first weekend in January'

The coalition government has spent much of the last year lamenting the lack of social mobility in this country of ours. Heaven alone knows what it might have made of rugby mobility, a rare phenomenon indeed in the elite club game since the introduction of a properly constituted national league system way back in 1987, when the Iron Lady was embarking on a third term in office and an iron No. 8 by the name of Buck Shelford was driving the All Blacks towards a first world

title. Twenty-three years on, there had been only five English champions: three of them – Bath, Leicester, Wasps – multiple winners; two of them, Newcastle and Sale, fly-by-nights of the one-off variety. Plus ça change, and all that.

Under the circumstances, Saracens were a godsend last season. Not everyone likes the cut of their jib – the South African influence, the agitprop tendencies (largely concealed after the in-your-face approach of the previous term, but still there), the risk-free policy that defined Mark McCall's first season as director of rugby – and it may be that Leicester, narrowly beaten by the Watford-based club in another memorable grand final at Twickenham, have less time for them than most, but the Premiership, now under the sponsorship of Aviva, badly needed a fresh name on its honours board.

Saracens lost their opening game – a meeting with London Irish at Twickenham as part of the annual London double-header – but it was transparently obvious by the end of September that they were serious contenders for the title they had been within seconds of winning last time out. Their victory over Northampton at Vicarage Road in round four told those with eyes to see everything they needed to know, for the Saints travelled down the M1 with an über-pack that had recently laid waste to both Leicester and Bath. The home side, magnificently led by the misused and ritually abused Steve Borthwick, took on the Midlanders at close quarters, won the arm-wrestle and earned Derick Hougaard more than enough shots at goal to clinch the deal.

To their enormous credit, Saracens carried on clinching for the rest of the campaign, losing a mere four games in total and none at all after the first weekend in January. The loss of Brendan Venter, the World Cup-winning Springbok centre, midway through the piece – he felt obliged to return to South Africa for family reasons and bequeathed the running of the operation to McCall – seemed like a desperate blow, but Venter promised to make the most of a new brief as technical adviser and was true to his word, contributing on an almost daily basis from his remote base in Cape Town and flying back

to England for matches or important training sessions a couple of times a month. To Venter's great satisfaction, the spirit of togetherness he summoned in his first season at Sarries survived his absences in the second. If ever there was proof of the value of his creation, this was it.

True, there were few glimpses of the counterattacking brilliance that had lifted Saracens' rugby so far above the ordinary in the final third of the 2009-10 season, although the try scored by Schalk Brits against Gloucester in April was utterly jaw-dropping: a multi-faceted coat-of-many-colours job that covered the length of the field, showcasing the very best of David Strettle, Owen Farrell and James Short as well as Brits, quite possibly the most gifted footballing forward in all the rugby-playing world. But there were legitimate reasons for this narrowing of the horizons, not least the feeling amongst most professional players that refereeing interpretations at the tackle area had tilted back, ever so slightly but enough, towards the defending side.

Also, the emergence of the teenaged Farrell at outside half forced them to think carefully about their modus operandi. Farrell was spectacularly impressive, but he did not arrive fully formed. He was brilliant in defence, as were Saracens to a man, and blessed with an instinctive understanding of the pulse and rhythm of a contest, but Farrell's running game was not quite of the same quality. This, together with the decision to play the indefatigable Jacques Burger as a destructive open-side flanker rather than employ the wide-ranging continuity skills of Andy Saull, ensured a tighter, more conservative brand of rugby.

Borthwick, whose demotion from the England senior squad a few weeks before the start of the season had been cruel and callous in equal measure, managed the new realities with his customary resourcefulness. As Venter said of him after that terrific victory over Northampton, 'He's exceptionally important to us. His ability to change things during the course of a game is fantastic. When Northampton cottoned on to what we were doing at the early line outs, he made small alterations that allowed us to improve in that area. It takes an old head to do that.' A few months later, Borthwick's running of the Sarries line out – not to mention his countless contributions elsewhere – would have a decisive say in the destination of the silverware.

FACING PAGE Ben Cohen in action for Sale Sharks against Leeds Carnegie at Edgeley Park. Both sides struggled in the Premiership, Leeds eventually falling through the trap door into the Championship. Cohen retired at the end of the season to launch his StandUp Foundation against bullying.

BELOW Flanker Tom Johnson scores for Exeter Chiefs against Newcastle Falcons. New boys Exeter made a good impression, finishing their first Premiership season in eighth place.

Saracens, Northampton, Leicester – at the start of term, these were the obvious heavyweight challengers. Many people thought Bath would join them in the mix, their judgment swayed by the riches bestowed upon the West Countrymen by new owner Bruce Craig, but money is no guarantee of overnight success, no matter how much of it a club can lay its hands on. An ageing tight-forward unit and problems with the midfield balance, allied to the failure to compensate for the wounding departures of Joe Maddock and Julian Salvi, made life something of a trial, particularly pre-Christmas.

With cash-strapped London Irish struggling with injuries – there was no fit open-side flanker available to them at one point and they lost six Premiership games in succession between late November and mid-February – and Wasps, even more challenged on the financial front, barely raising a trot, let alone a gallop, it was left to Gloucester and Harlequins to gatecrash the big boys' party. Both were fun to watch: they backed their home-grown talent, they played the game at pace, they generated memorable atmospheres when performing at home. Forgive the heresy, but these two clubs have more in common than they would like to admit.

BELOW Left wing James Short goes over for Saracens in the 29th minute for the only try of the final.

FACING PAGE Saracens make the most of their first Premiership title win.

There was an additional joy, and it came from an unfamiliar neck of the union woods. While the three northern clubs were trying, and failing, to make sense of life in the top echelon of English rugby – Sale were a basket case, Newcastle as forlorn as they were anonymous, Leeds almost entirely devoid of hope as well as merit – the newcomers from Exeter had themselves a ball. Cleverly coached by Rob Baxter, whose sound grasp of the basics proved invaluable, Devon's finest

began Premiership life with a home victory over Gloucester, put the fear of God up Leicester at Welford Road a week later and went onwards and upwards from there. But for an entirely profligate performance at Leeds, they would have won half their matches and finished the season all-square. As it was, they ended it comfortably placed in eighth position, ahead of two former champions, and with plans afoot for further stadium development at Sandy Park, not to mention a bold refinancing scheme that will allow them to buy the Premiership shares currently held by Bristol, there is more than a whiff of long-termism about them.

If the collapse of the northern sector raised fears over the viability of professional club rugby as a nationwide concern, it was not the only cause for unease. Again, there was a football-style turnover of head coaches: Steve Meehan left Bath under a cloud while Tony Hanks, Mike Brewer and Andy Key were sacked by Wasps, Sale and Leeds respectively. Again, there was widespread alarm at refereeing standards. Again, a number of high-profile players misbehaved in the most boneheaded ways imaginable, both on and off the field. And again, there was unrest on the financial front. By no means all the Premiership clubs, or even a simple majority, are happy with the latest tinkerings on the salary cap front, which will allow more expenditure on players from the start of next season.

But as ever, the rugby itself saved the day. The Saracens v Leicester final did not touch the free-running, try-scoring heights of the 2010 decider between the same sides, but as a piece of sporting theatre, it gripped from the start and refused to let go. Borthwick, Brits, Burger – truly, the 'Killer Bs' – were majestic in their determination to wrest the trophy from the Tigers, never less so than at the last knockings, when Jordan Crane and his fellow Midlanders initiated a goal-line siege that lasted seven minutes and 32 phases. Four points up at 22-18, Saracens were one missed tackle away from a second successive injury-time defeat. Never once, even when faced with the seemingly interminable and inevitable, did they look like missing anything.

It is too early to say whether that epic defensive effort marked the start of a new era of domination, but it certainly ended the old one. And that can only be a good thing.

Farrell & Son
a Saracens Dynasty

by STEVE BALE

'Owen has World Cups to come. But that was it for Andy, who had little chance once his belated union career had been overwhelmed by his repeated inability to get on the field'

The contrast between how the Farrells, son and father, were received into rugby union is complete and explains why young Owen is likely to achieve vastly more in the 15-a-side game than his rugby-league legend of a dad ever did. When Andy Farrell joined Saracens from Wigan in 2006, he was already 30 years of age and inevitably northern wiseacres took the cynical view he had dodgy knees so was anyway at the end of his usefulness as a league man. Successive England coaches, Andy Robinson and Brian Ashton, did not see it that way and never yielded to criticism that Farrell had come to union too late to warrant the £1.5 million investment shared between his new club and the RFU. Ultimately Farrell senior added eight union caps to the 34 for Great Britain and 11 for England that he gained in league. Had he crossed the divide earlier, and been unplagued by the injuries which followed his crossing, who knows?

Owen Farrell, on the other hand, was made to go south with his father and, having given up an inevitably promising league career, became the youngest professional union player in England on his Saracens debut against Llanelli Scarlets in the EDF Energy Cup in October 2008. It was natural he would pick up an ovoid, not a spheroid. 'I am my own person and I don't expect anything from anyone,' he said. 'It was natural I would take to rugby because I always had a ball in my hand.'

If you are 17 years and 11 days old, as he was against the Scarlets, your rugby life lies ahead of you, not behind. We have seen in the culmination of the 2010-11 season, and Farrell's pivotal role in Saracens winning the Premiership title, what even two years can do. 'Every time a new challenge is

presented to Owen, he has risen to that challenge,' said his club coach Mark McCall. 'For a guy in his first year out of school to play with this composure and control is a remarkable performance.'

McCall was referring not only to Farrell's dead-eyed goal-kicking performance in Saracens' defeat of Leicester in the Premiership final last May, though even as a one-off it was an astounding contribution for a teenage fly half. For McCall it was more the progress his young man had made over the course of an entire season, because it was unexpected even to the most admiring of Farrell's coaches. They had, after all, seen fit to send him out to Bedford last September.

Farrell received his Saracens opportunity only because events did not transpire as the club had intended. First, the trumpeted move of Alex Goode from full back to fly half did not work out in accordance with the plan. Goode was long since back at full back by the time Saracens were beating Leicester at Twickenham. Saracens had also been without their Springbok fly half Derick Hougaard for almost all the season after a ruptured Achilles tendon last October.

ABOVE Owen Farrell hands off to Brad Barritt during the Aviva Premiership semi-final between Saracens and Gloucester. Farrell landed four penalties in Sarries' 12-10 win.

FACING PAGE Coach Farrell senior tosses the kicking tee to Farrell junior at Twickenham as Saracens beat Leicester to claim their first Premiership.

So Farrell's inclusion was more emergency than pre-ordained. Yet he providentially turned out to be 'a kid who played like a man', to borrow the memorable description used by Saracens' South African hooker Schalk Brits. You could see this at least as much in Saracens' Premiership semi-final victory over Gloucester as in his impeccable final. It was Farrell's decisive late penalty which sealed a 12-10 win, when he had already missed four. As a question about temperament, it was strongly answered in the affirmative. Including the final, Saracens won 13 straight Premiership fixtures, a fine record that would have been impossible without their youngest player.

'It says everything that he misses some kicks and then puts his hand up to kick the winning penalty,' McCall said. 'He has been incredible for us over a six-month period. He has guided us to this run of victories.'

It is true to say Andy Farrell did not receive such overwhelming acclaim when he was being picked for England, as was excruciatingly demonstrated at the 2007 World Cup. By the time England reached the final, he had succumbed to a calf injury. Owen has World Cups to come, and played for England and was a finalist at the junior version in Italy in June. But that was it for Andy, who had little chance once his belated union career had been overwhelmed by his repeated inability to get on the field. This was a league player of the greatest distinction, possibly the very greatest Englishman who ever played the game. Some people evidently considered this was all the qualification needed to make a success of union.

It is perhaps cruel now to recall what occurred after England were thrashed 36-0 by South Africa in their RWC 2007 pool. England's defence coach Mike Ford, himself a GB league cap, sadly reflected on how Farrell's persistent absences had affected his rugby. 'Twelve months out have done him no favours,' Ford said. 'He is getting to grips with it but probably too late, with his age, to be where he wants to be. It's not that simple to say we aren't using him the best we can.'

In other words, the 'fault' lay with England generally as well as with Farrell, by then 32. For all his wonderful rugby-playing ability, he had not enjoyed any of the considerable advantages being given his no-less-talented son Owen four years on. A few days later the England management, tacitly embarrassed at Ford's honest candour, sought to rewrite history with a perverse press release in which the same Mike Ford heaped praise on Andy Farrell. 'What we are seeing now is that he is getting better and better with every game,' Ford was quoted as saying. 'I feel he will have an impact on this tournament and even after the World Cup he has at least another two years at the top level.'

Spot the difference. Andy is now mentoring Owen, and everyone else in the champion Saracens squad, as one of McCall's co-coaches, with the evidence indicating he is doing a terrific job both individually and collectively.

As it happens, Owen Farrell later lost his record as the youngest English rugby union professional to one George Ford of Leicester, who was 16 years and 237 days old on his Tigers debut and latterly an England junior World Cup finalist alongside Owen.

That's the son of the self-same Mike Ford.

Pirates Ahoy!
Cornwall Eyes the Premiership
by NEALE HARVEY

'If the stadium plan flies, we'll stay full-time and attack the Premiership. But if the stadium doesn't fly then that's it, we're back to the dark ages'

At a highly charged and emotional supporters' meeting in April 2005, the driving force behind Penzance & Newlyn RFC, president Dicky Evans, outlined his exciting vision of the future for Cornwall's leading club in their quest to reach English rugby's top tier. The West Cornwall side had, Evans insisted, reached a 'watershed' in its history and the time had come for change.

Evans' controversial plan included changing the club's name to the Cornish Pirates, forming a new company – Penzance & Newlyn Rugby Limited – and relocating the playing base from the Mennaye Field in Penzance to a site near Truro, bang in the middle of the Duchy. Hailing his rebranded Pirates as 'The Team for Cornwall', Evans, a former Penzance & Newlyn player, boldly declared, 'Cornish rugby is a sleeping giant and now is the time to awaken that giant. We are a Premiership club in waiting and this is the time for us to finally move forward and realise our dream.'

The proposal sparked consternation amongst certain dyed-in-the-wool traditionalists, some of whom demanded the club should retain its old name and stay put. A few angry souls even walked out in disgust, vowing never to return. But Evans remained defiant in the face of his critics, steadfastly insisting, 'To realise our dream it is simply not possible to do this as we are. Penwith has a catchment area of 130,000 people, central Cornwall has a catchment area of 500,000. To move this club is tearing me apart, but we have to be realistic.'

Evans was right. Having helped drag the club up through six levels of rugby in eight years – from the Western Counties to National League One (now the RFU Championship) –

ABOVE Cornish Pirates owner and former Penzance & Newlyn player Dicky Evans remains hopeful that a stadium can be built and Premiership rugby brought to Cornwall.

since returning to his roots to take ownership of Penzance & Newlyn in 1995, the Kenya-based business tycoon knew that in order to progress to the top flight the club had to think big. Remaining at the atmospheric but ill-equipped Mennaye Field was not an option if the ultimate dream was to be realised.

Evans got his way and the move paid off. The newly named Cornish Pirates moved to a temporary stadium at Kenwyn, outside Truro, in time for the start of season 2005-06 and crowds doubled overnight as the people of Cornwall bought into Evans' vision. A successful first season saw the club achieve its highest ever league placing – third in the league, fifteenth in the country overall – and with crowds averaging 3000, the potential for the Pirates was clear for all to see.

But whilst that progress on the pitch has been maintained, not everything has gone to plan off it. Having lifted the EDF National Trophy by beating the Exeter Chiefs at Twickenham in April 2007, the Pirates decamped again to play at the Recreation Ground in Camborne, a move prompted by the high running costs associated with maintaining a temporary ground upcountry. Financial issues were later exacerbated by the economic downturn, causing Evans to rein in his spending further and return the club to its spiritual home in Penzance for the start of last season.

But the ambition remains undimmed and having captured the inaugural British & Irish Cup by beating Munster in May 2010, the Pirates again came to national prominence this year by running the Worcester Warriors close in the Championship play-off final. Talented players like scrum half Gavin Cattle and fly half Jonny Bentley were provided with a platform to showcase their skills in front of the Sky cameras and did not let anybody down as Chris Stirling's side gave the Warriors a full and honest workout before losing the two-legged tie 46-32 on aggregate.

The appointment of Stirling as High Performance Manager in January 2009 has proved to be an inspired decision by Evans, who had been keen to build on the previous good work done by Jim McKay, the amiable Australian who established the club as a force in second-tier rugby before moving on to roles at Leicester Tigers and the Queensland Reds. Stirling, a New Zealander who had cut his teeth in coaching at club level at home and built a reputation for attention to detail, arrived with the remit of developing a team capable of challenging for a place in the Premiership.

He has certainly achieved that. In collaboration with former Wasps scrum half Harvey Biljon, who looks after the attack, and forwards coach Ian Davies, a Level 4-qualified coach

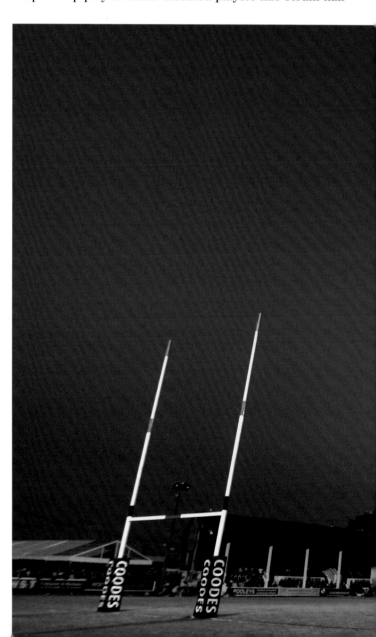

RIGHT Evening settles over the Mennaye Field, Penzance, during the 2010-11 RFU Championship play-off final first leg between Cornish Pirates and Worcester Warriors.

who learnt his trade lower down the National League system at Worthing, Stirling has fashioned a highly committed side that is both good to watch and mightily effective when it comes to the business of winning rugby matches. The Pirates ended the 2010-11 regular season in third place before scooting through the play-offs, averaging four tries and 30 points per match along the way. Little wonder the people at Sky became regular visitors to the Mennaye Field from Christmas onwards.

So, whither the Cornish Pirates? The team looks fine, there is no problem there and Stirling has made nine close-season signings, including some with Premiership experience such as winger David Doherty (ex-Leeds, Wasps and Sale) and Leeds fly half Ceiron Thomas (previously of Llanelli Scarlets), along with acquiring four further players on dual registration from Premiership outfit Exeter Chiefs. But the big issue is the stadium, or lack of it, because without a new 10,000-capacity arena the dream of bringing Premiership rugby to Cornwall is dead. Evans knows it, the players know it and the fans know it, which is why the race is on to get a purpose-built stadium up and running for season 2012-13.

The big anticlimax of last season's otherwise enthralling Championship campaign came with the knowledge that of the four sides competing in the play-off semi-finals, only Worcester had a Premiership-standard ground. The other three, including the Pirates, were effectively playing for pride, an anomaly that Evans and his cohorts are desperate to correct. The aim, therefore, is to

develop a new 'Stadium for Cornwall' in Truro, at the very heart of the Duchy, which would enable Stirling's team to take the field this season confident in the knowledge that a place in the top flight would be theirs if they could go a step further and win the play-off final.

It is all or nothing, and the Pirates have been working closely with Cornwall Council since 2010 to bring the project to fruition. A bullish Evans explained, 'The Pirates have reached another watershed. We're going to have to get a move on and start attacking the Premiership. I've been funding the club since 1995 and we are where we are, but there's an opportunity now to take this club forward. If the Council can provide agreement on a new stadium and planning permission is in place, we can definitely make Premiership rugby happen. I've got to commit to the new stadium for ten years, which I will do, and then all I'm asking is for supporters to be part of this scheme as well so that we can attack the Premiership next season and try to win promotion.'

Evans believes that Premiership rugby is both deliverable and sustainable in Cornwall, one of the game's few genuine hotbeds in the country, and he has been taking soundings over the level of support the Pirates might enjoy once they reach the Promised Land. The numbers stack up, with crowds of 10,000 achievable, but if the project fails a doomsday scenario could unfold. Evans warned, 'If the stadium plan flies, we'll stay full-time and attack the Premiership. But if the stadium doesn't fly then that's it, we're back to the dark ages and that's the end of bringing Premiership rugby to Cornwall. That is the stark reality of the situation, I'm afraid, and the future would be pretty bleak.'

It is knife-edge stuff down in Cornwall, and the future of the Cornish Pirates lies very much in the hands of the Council planners, who can either see off any local opposition and share the vision for a much-needed Stadium for Cornwall – a multi-purpose, privately funded venue which would most likely be used jointly by the Pirates and the equally ambitious Truro City Football Club – or condemn the Duchy to being a sporting backwater for the foreseeable future, or maybe even forever.

Do they have that vision? They ought to, because across the River Tamar the Exeter Chiefs have shown what is possible in the rugby-mad Southwest with some careful long-term planning and a burning desire to bring top-class sport to the region. The Cornish public's appetite for Premiership rugby is arguably greater than that of their erstwhile rivals from Devon, where the ambitious Chiefs attracted regular crowds of 10,000-plus during their inaugural Premiership campaign.

Early autumn is when planning issues are set to become clearer, but Pirates chief executive Rod Coward said, 'I think we've got a real prospect of advancing now in terms of facilities and if everything comes together fairly quickly, a stadium could be delivered for the start of season 2012-13. It's do-able if all things fit together.'

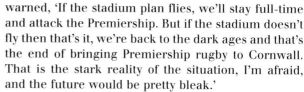

LEFT Cornish Kiwi Jonny Bentley runs away from covering Warriors during the Championship play-off final first leg at 'The Mennaye'. The stand-off forms a talented half-back pairing with skipper Gavin Cattle.

Jonny Turns the Tide
the 2010-11 Heineken Cup

by DAVID HANDS

'Sexton, it emerged later, had been one of those to offer the most inspirational words in the changing room at half-time, and by the time he departed he had matched action to words'

Ireland have held the whip hand over England for much of the last international decade and now they have extended their grip to the Heineken Cup. In 2009, Leinster claimed their first European title by beating Leicester, and in 2011 the Irish province took their second against the other East Midland giant, Northampton. Set in one context, of course, an English representative in the final in Cardiff was significant. There had been gripes and groans during 2009-10 that English clubs were underperforming, that they were suffering in contrast to their French and Celtic cousins because of the self-imposed salary cap which limited squad size and star quality. In that season, Northampton were the only English side to reach the quarter-finals, and that was the extent of their success; this year they were joined by Leicester in the last eight, alongside four French clubs and two Irish provinces, which seemed to suggest that the doom-mongers had a point.

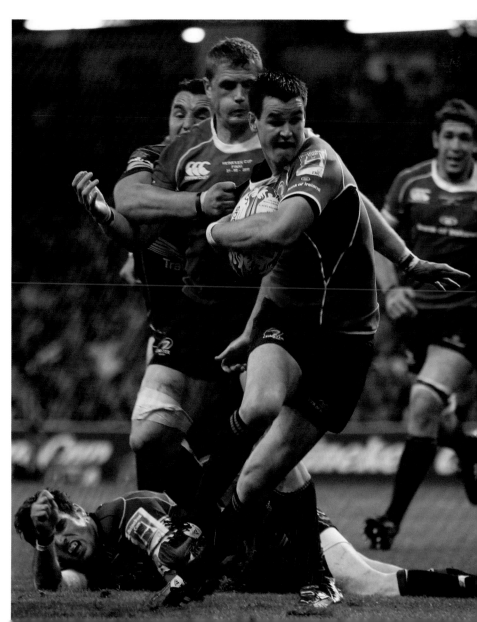

RIGHT Leinster outside half Jonny Sexton on his way to the Northampton line for his second try of the 2011 Heineken Cup final at the Millennium Stadium. Sexton scored no fewer than 28 of Leinster's 33 points.

But the French fell by the wayside, most notably four-times winners Toulouse, who crashed to Leinster in the semi-finals. Given that, in the previous round, Leinster had disposed of Leicester, the English champions, no one can cavil at their reclaiming the title with a tenacity that only confirmed how well they have banished the accusations of flakiness – once their critics' watchword.

But how hard they made it for themselves. There has not been a final like that at the Millennium Stadium, where the pendulum swung so far one way in the first half, and so far the other way in the second. At the interval, Northampton (winners of the Heineken Cup in 2000) led 22-6 and had played some of their best rugby of the season; then Leinster emerged and washed their English opponents away in a flood of 27 unanswered points to win 33-22. It was what the Northampton management had feared. 'We had put everything we had into that first half,' said assistant coach Dorian West, himself a Heineken Cup winner with Leicester ten years earlier. 'Looking in some of their faces, they were tired.'

They had reason to be, because the imbalance in game time remains: whereas English Premiership clubs face a demanding season involving three domestic tournaments, as well as international calls, the Irish – with no relegation from the Celtic league – are able to manage their leading players that much better. One estimate, in the week leading up to the final, suggested that the playing commitments of Leinster's stars were around 30 per cent less than those of Northampton.

The previous weekend, Northampton had been pounded by Leicester in the Aviva Premiership play-off, a typically physical encounter, whereas Leinster had an extra 24 hours to recover from the Magners League play-off victory over Ulster and the scope to rest some significant individuals. The demands proved too much for Northampton, and the player who did most to open them up was Jonathan Sexton, the Ireland fly half. Having knocked over Leinster's two first-half penalty goals, Sexton scored the two tries in the third quarter – and kicked the goals – which put Leinster ahead.

Sexton, it emerged later, had been one of those to offer the most inspirational words in the changing room at half-time, and by the time he departed he had matched action to words and scored 28 points, including the conversion of a try by Nathan Hines which finished Northampton off. By then, the Saints' first-half supremacy was a faint memory: the accuracy of Stephen Myler, Northampton's No. 10, counted for nothing, though he had contributed so much to the tries scored by Phil Dowson, Ben Foden and Dylan Hartley.

The challenge for Northampton is to build on the experience, as Munster had to do before they won the cup; as Leicester did too. Leinster, though, are not short of youth. Back-row forward Sean O'Brien, who turned 24 during the campaign, was the revelation of the Irish season, and the likes of Sexton, Luke Fitzgerald and Cian Healy (aged 25, 23 and 23 respectively during the 2010-11 season) already have great experience and a future still before them.

Northampton, in fact, kicked off the 2010-11 tournament with a laboured home win over Castres. It was hardly a game in which they served notice of intent, though with hindsight it hinted at the demise of the French challenge. France had seven representatives, more than any other country, but none was left standing seven months later.

It is understandable that a side such as Racing Métro 92, newly promoted to the Top 14, should have concentrated on domestic affairs. The same is true for Toulon, for all their overseas players, but the other five clubs should possess wider ambitions. True, the quarter-final draw did them no favours, since it produced two all-French games, both of them minor classics.

Biarritz came from behind against Toulouse in San Sebastián, overhauled a 17-point deficit to force extra time and then lost to a charge-down try by Yannick Nyanga. Perpignan, for their part, also took their game with Toulon to Spain and played in front of 55,000 at the Olympic Stadium in Barcelona. At the interval they trailed 11-6, but their second-half charge carried them to a wildly celebrated 29-25 win in which the critical try was scored by Perry Freshwater, the former England prop.

The writing was on the wall for the representatives of Italy, Scotland and Wales even before the final round of pool matches – no surprise so far as the first two countries were concerned but the source of grave disappointment in Wales where the failure of Cardiff Blues and Ospreys to win home games cooked their goose. Ospreys, to be fair, were in a pool with Toulon, London Irish and Munster, the last-mentioned providing the shock of the season by failing to reach the knockout phase for the first time in 13 years. Munster have been one of the perennial greats during the 16 years of the Heineken Cup, the best-followed of teams, who have made of their Thomond Park ground in Limerick a fortress. However, they opened with defeat in Reading against London Irish, suffered the dismissal of Paul O'Connell, the 2009 Lions captain, during the home win over Ospreys and crashed 32-16 to Toulon in the Stade Félix Mayol. Only a devastating final ten minutes earned them their home win in the return fixture with London Irish, which might have been a portent, since on their descent to the Amlin Challenge Cup, they lost at home to Harlequins.

Not that Munster were the only notable casualties when the dust settled on the pool stage. London Wasps, twice champions, might have won in Toulouse had not a penalty attempt by David Walder slid wide of an upright, but their hopes crumbled in a 20-10 away defeat to Glasgow Warriors; not even a home win over Toulouse (which cost the French club a home quarter-final) could console them.

Bath, the first English Heineken champions in 1998, never dredged up enough consistent form, while both London Irish and Saracens finished bottom of their respective pools. Given that Saracens went on to become domestic champions four months later, their return of one win in six games was disappointing and concluded an unhappy relationship for the season with European Rugby Cup Ltd, the tournament organisers.

Saracens had been fined 5000 Euros for the failure of Steve Borthwick, the captain, to attend the Heineken Cup launch, which clashed with a club visit to the Munich beer festival; a further penalty of 25,000 Euros was imposed for critical comments about refereeing made by Brendan Venter (then the director of rugby) after Saracens lost to Leinster at Wembley. Venter, angered by the fine, gave a bizarre post-match interview on television after Saracens had lost at home to Racing Métro in the next round. Offering only monosyllabic responses or repeating the interviewer's questions, Venter's action was ascribed to his anxiety not to plunge into any more hot water, and ERC confined their response, this time, to a warning about his future conduct.

Northampton, meanwhile, came through their pool unbeaten, whereas Leicester had to concede first place to Perpignan and qualify for the last eight as one of the best runners-up. Perpignan's scrum damaged the Tigers badly at the Stade Aimé Giral, and Leicester could only draw the return fixture the following weekend on a day when Billy Twelvetrees, the highly rated young centre, landed five penalties and a conversion but missed four other kicks. The result, or lack of one, cost the Tigers a home quarter-final, and Leinster rubbed home the advantage of playing at the Aviva Stadium in Dublin. Northampton, meanwhile, enjoyed the benefits of playing both their quarter-final against Ulster and their semi-final against Perpignan at stadium:mk, the functional new headquarters of MK Dons down the road at Milton Keynes.

On both occasions, the power of the home forwards (Roger Wilson, the No. 8, playing against his old Ulster team-mates) proved decisive. But when it came to the final, they could not out-muscle the Leinster pack, hardened by wins over Leicester and Toulouse and assisted by the ability of Brian O'Driscoll, even on days when his all-round standards dropped, to produce moments of match-winning magic.

Leo Cullen: the Quiet Leader

by SEAN DIFFLEY

'The squad may contain more celebrated figures in Brian O'Driscoll and Jonny Sexton, but it is the more reserved Cullen who mans the helm'

A powerhouse line-out operator is how a match programme has described Leo Cullen, but such his Leinster team-mates would disdain as totally insufficient. Captain of Leinster for the third successive season and leader in the Heineken Cup triumph in 2011, Cullen has made contributions that are far more extensive. He is a quiet leader, never given to many outpourings to the media, but he has the total respect of his Leinster squad, a happy ship who recognise his serene but so effective influence in all aspects. The squad may contain more celebrated figures in Brian O'Driscoll and Jonny Sexton, but it is the more reserved Cullen who mans the helm, his quiet influence recognised as a major factor in that remarkable second-half revival to beat Northampton in the Heineken final.

Leo Cullen, of course, got the best possible grounding. He was at school at Blackrock College, the famed, all-successful nursery which has produced such British & Irish Lions as Fergus Slattery, Niall Brophy and the versatile Hugo MacNeill. Blackrock has dominated the Leinster Schools Cup competitions down the years

LEFT May 21 2011. Leinster captain Leo Cullen gets his hands on the Heineken Cup for the second time in three years. The following month he was celebrating again – on that occasion his marriage.

and Leo has been involved, being in the Under 15 winning team in 1993 and then in the senior side (Under 18) which won in 1995 and again the following season. An interesting footnote to that 1996 win was that someone got it classically wrong: on the bench and taking no part with his Blackrock schoolmates in the final was a certain Brian O'Driscoll.

During those schooldays, too, Cullen was for two seasons in the Irish Schools team; he went on to represent Ireland Under 19, Under 21 and Under 25 before getting his first full Ireland cap in Auckland against the All Blacks in 2002. Cullen came on as a replacement on that occasion and has figured as a replacement in more than half of his subsequent 28 matches for Ireland. The opposition in his position has been fierce: Paul O'Connell, Donncha O'Callaghan, Michael O'Driscoll and Malcolm O'Kelly. But after this significant year, with its Heineken European Cup victory and his all-round display and contribution, all the signs are that Cullen's stature has clearly grown, although at 33 years old he is perhaps entering the twilight of his career.

Cullen went to Leicester Tigers in 2004 and was a highly respected and popular member of that fine team. He returned to Leinster in 2007, winning the Magner's League with them in his first season back. Then came Leinster's great breakthrough with their first Heineken victory in 2009, with Cullen as captain. Until this point Leinster had not rated as tough enough, physically or mentally, and suffered, humbly, in comparison with the all-successful Munster. But the situation has altered, and there has been a great change of attitude as Leinster have proved themselves one of the very best sides in the northern hemisphere. While coaches and some players have been the beneficiaries of general praise, the contribution of the captain Leo Cullen is very clear to the discerning, including his own players.

LEFT Cullen, in the green shirt of Ireland, battles with Quintin Geldenhuys of Italy at Croke Park during the 2010 Six Nations.

Quins By a Whisker
the 2011 Challenge Cup Final

by TERRY COOPER

'It left Evans with an apparently awkward kick from the right-hand side and just over halfway out to win the match. Awkward? Not for one of the supreme kickers of the modern game'

The normal order for this century in Europe's second-tier event was restored when Harlequins again stole the Challenge Cup with another last-gasp victory against French opposition. At Cardiff City Stadium, Stade Français followed Narbonne (2001) and Montferrand (2004) in losing to a late, unexpected, decisive assault by Quins, who underlined former coach Dick Best's law: 'We are in love with cup rugby'.

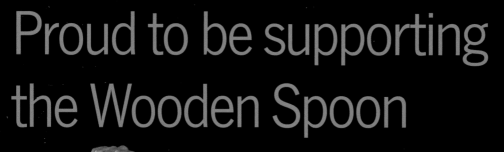

When Argentina's Gonzalo Camacho bounced over for the game's solitary try with three minutes left and nerveless Nick Evans added the winning conversion, it was the ninth success in this event for English clubs in the last 11 seasons. The roll reads: Quins (three titles), Sale (two), Wasps, Gloucester, Bath and Northampton.

Stade were appearing in their third Euro final, having lost twice in the Heineken Cup. Unfortunately for them, on every occasion they neglected to score a try. Costly, especially this time, when victory in Cardiff was their only route to qualifying for the Heineken after a ropey season in domestic combat in which they finished eleventh in the Top 14. Unthinkable relegation had loomed.

Close observers always gave Quins a chance against the Parisian favourites. The evidence was strong. They had no fear of the opposition, having beaten them home and away in the Heineken two years before. Quins had been hard to defeat all season, though they had failed to qualify for the Heineken by league position. In the Amlin, they had succeeded gloriously in the knockout stages at home against Wasps (32-22) then away to Munster (20-12), both matches against recent Heineken champions. And any perceived French superiority at all levels of rugby still can fade to nothing when they cross the Channel.

The contest pretty much defined the phrase 'slow burner'. Harlequins shaded the first half 9-6 with a trio of penalties for Evans against a couple from Lionel Beauxis, his first being a mighty

ABOVE Stade Français No. 8 and captain Sergio Parisse finds himself in some space during the Amlin Challenge Cup final at Cardiff City Stadium.

PAGE 93 Nick Evans slots the conversion of Gonzalo Camacho's late try to win the cup for Harlequins.

ABOVE Stade's chunky France centre Mathieu Bastareaud thumps over a left-footed dropped goal on 47 minutes.

FACING PAGE Skipper Chris Robshaw holds high the trophy as Harlequins become the first club to win the Challenge competition three times.

thump from 60 yards. Between Evans' third strike in the 27th minute and the breathtaking finale, Quins were the junior partners, conceding scores and barely hanging on, though the defence was immaculate. Untypically, Nick Easter epitomised Quins' long spell in the shadows with handling errors and penalty concessions. He was thoroughly outplayed by his rival No. 8, classy Sergio Parisse, Italy's captain. By the hour, Stade led 15-9 with Beauxis' third and fourth penalties either side of a dropped goal from centre Mathieu Bastareaud. Evans failed with one penalty shortly before collecting another. But Stade seemed to have settled the argument at 18-12 in the 72nd minute when full back Martín Rodríguez gathered a missed clearance kick by Evans and fired home a prodigious drop kick from 50 yards.

Against all expectations, Harlequins created a surging move that splintered the Stade defence. It started with full back Mike Brown, who had been a rare beacon in attack and defence during the French side's time in charge. Easter then contributed twice, and progress was maintained by props Joe Gray and Joe Marler and centre Jordan Turner-Hall. Danny Care entered to give the attack a defining twist by prodding through a shrewd, perfectly weighted diagonal kick off his left foot to wing Camacho, who gathered it safely and brushed tacklers aside for the try. It left Evans with an apparently awkward kick from the right-hand side and just over halfway out to win the match. Awkward? Not for one of the supreme kickers of the modern game. Over it went. 19-18 to Quins. Evans attributed his accuracy under pressure to the work ethic. 'That's why all the kickers in world rugby spend so many extra hours on the training pitch.'

With triumph a mere couple of minutes away, Quins had to withstand a scrum in a dangerous position straight from Stade's kick-off. They were helped by referee George Clancy, who barked, like a sergeant major, 'Use it' five times as Stade held the ball in the back row. Of course, being reluctantly forced to use it they promptly proceeded to lose it, ending the match. It was a strange command by Clancy, but then the scrum is becoming the bête noire of rugby. Parisse justifiably complained long and loud, arguing that it was Stade's scrum, their ball and they were entitled to manoeuvre for a penalty, a drop kick or a strike position without having their tactic foisted on them.

Director of rugby Michael Cheika did not like it one bit. He tried to restrain himself but failed. 'We are devastated. We deserved better. Once again we came undone due to the shortcomings of [pause] … I don't think I should say, because I could get in trouble.' Then instinct kicked in. 'The referee took away our advantage in the second half in the areas where we dominated. One decision at a scrum when we were pushing them back was a joke. Sergio was very upset. It's big stakes.' But by the time he uttered these words he was already in trouble and was later cited for allegedly making offensive and insulting comments to match and ERC officials.

James Haskell nobly took the blame for the try. 'My gut feeling is that it was my fault, by coming out of the defensive line, that Harlequins scored. I will not sleep too well tonight. It's pretty difficult for me to take.' Haskell suspected that he was already one of the players about to be released as Stade tried to do something about their £5 million-plus debt.

Quins captain Easter had to be realistic when he commented through his winning grin, 'We were very poor in the second half and did not control the game. We needed that never-say-die spirit.'

Director of rugby Conor O'Shea added, 'We needed only seven points after that drop goal, so the lights were never out in the final stages. We have been on the end of some heartbreaking defeats this season. Now it's our turn to inflict one on Stade. We played in the wrong part of the pitch as Stade caught and overtook us, but we hung on and finally got an offloading game going successfully.

The team decided the way they wanted to play at the start of the season. We were far from that ambitious style tonight, but in the final the overriding aim was to win the silverware. Did we play poorly? Yes, but who cares? We have lost by three, four and five points during the season, but we are always battering away near the end. When you beat Bayonne, Munster and Wasps on the way to a final you develop some self-belief. We've played well enough throughout all the campaigns to deserve a bit of luck. We had nine fellows there aged 25 or under and this will give them a mental boost about where we can go from this win.'

Harlequins emerged from a pool that included Connacht, Bayonne and I Cavalieri Estra, before beating Wasps in the quarter-final and stunning Munster in the last four; Stade's group contained Bucharest Oaks, Leeds and Italy's Crociati Rugby, and the Parisians then had narrow wins over Montpellier (32-28) and Clermont Auvergne (29-25) in the knockout rounds.

Destination Kingsholm
the 2010-11 LV= Cup

by **PAUL BOLTON**

'Robinson's most crucial contribution came when he twice offloaded to Eliota Fuimaono-Sapolu in the build-up to the Samoan international centre's brilliant 58th-minute try'

Gloucester ended a frustrating eight-year wait for a domestic title by sweeping aside a brave but outclassed Newcastle 34-7 in a high-tempo final at Franklin's Gardens. Gloucester's win ended a run of four defeats in finals (including the previous two in the Anglo-Welsh competition), stretched their unbeaten run to 11 matches in all competitions (their best sequence in 51 years) and secured them early qualification for the 2011-12 Heineken Cup.

BELOW Gloucester's England Saxons wing Charlie Sharples dives in for the third of his four tries against the Dragons in the LV= Cup semi-final at Kingsholm, which Gloucester won 45-17. Sharples was named in England's 45-man World Cup training squad in the summer.

In the build-up to the final, Gloucester head coach Bryan Redpath had appeared uncomfortable with his side's status as pre-match favourites and had warned his players against complacency. The former Scotland scrum half need not have worried. Thanks to a high-class display from fly half Nicky Robinson, Gloucester played the more composed rugby in a frenetic contest.

Robinson relieved the pressure with raking touch kicks and featured prominently in Gloucester's first three tries, cleverly changing the angle of attack or opening up Newcastle's defence with some sweetly timed passes. Robinson's most crucial contribution came when he twice offloaded to Eliota Fuimaono-Sapolu in the build-up to the Samoan international centre's brilliant 58th-minute try which finally broke Newcastle's resistance.

It was a bitter-sweet experience for Robinson – who also kicked 14 points – since he had already been informed by Redpath that Gloucester would not be renewing his contract. The former Wales international subsequently signed for London Wasps. 'It's tough for Nicky to move. But I'm pleased for him because he's shown great character and great composure at what has been a difficult time for him,' said Redpath.

'He got the man-of-the-match award too so whatever we remember Nicky for it will certainly be a day like this.

'The players stuck to a lot of basics. I thought Nicky's kicking to the bottom right-hand corner was exceptional and it just frustrated Newcastle.

'It gave us a bit of strength and then we took our opportunities. I am delighted for the players and the staff. I am absolutely chuffed to bits for everybody involved with the club.'

Just as they had against Harlequins in their semi-final, Newcastle defended heroically for long periods, but this time there was no one to conjure an improbable win. Jimmy Gopperth missed two first-half penalties which would at least have given them a glimmer of hope. Luke Eves's close-range try may have provided some consolation for Newcastle's loyal supporters, but by that stage Gloucester had thrown on most of their substitutes and were already celebrating winning the competition for the fifth time since it was introduced 40 years ago.

An early try created by Tim Molenaar for former England winger Tom Voyce, a regular trophy winner during his time with Wasps, should have settled Gloucester; instead they undid some promising approach work with clumsy errors until Robinson worked his magic with Fuimaono-Sapolu. 'We were very edgy for the first 50 minutes and a bit nervous and we just needed to calm down a bit,' Redpath admitted.

Once they had settled, Gloucester rammed home their superiority with further tries from Charlie Sharples and replacement hooker Darren Dawidiuk.

'I shook Bryan's hand after the game and the first thing I said to him was "It was probably a job too far for us",' said Newcastle head coach Alan Tait.

'Full credit to what they are doing at Gloucester. They looked the part even in the warm-up. They are a good outfit.

'Obviously ten games on the bounce is no mean feat, but we got stuck into the game and I still thought we had a bit of a chance at half-time because I knew we were still strong.

'We just didn't play in the right areas and when they got us to 20-0 we started to play the old Barbarian stuff that doesn't really work at this level.'

The finalists had contrasting passages through the semi-finals, with Gloucester romping to a 45-17 win over Newport Gwent Dragons at Kingsholm and Newcastle snatching a last-gasp 21-20 victory against Harlequins at the Twickenham Stoop.

Of Gloucester's seven tries against the Dragons, England Saxons wing Charlie Sharples rattled in three in 13 second-half minutes and added a fourth eight minutes later. His third was the best of them. Fijian flanker Akapusi Qera, unmarked at the tail of a line out, gathered and splintered the Dragons defence with a rampaging run before he delivered a perfect scoring pass to Sharples.

There was some good-natured mickey-taking from his team-mates when Sharples was announced as man of the match because it was very much a team performance. Yet it had taken some tough talking from Redpath at half-time to give Gloucester some focus after an error-riddled first-half performance. 'It was the worst performance we have had in ten weeks in the first 40 minutes by a country mile,' he said.

Newcastle, meanwhile, needed a try from replacement centre Tane Tu'ipulotu from the final play of the match to reach their first final in seven years. Tu'ipulotu crossed after two minutes of sustained pressure following a breakout by Gopperth, who had earlier scored an important opportunist try when he raced 70 metres after Karl Dickson had lost the ball in contact. At one stage it looked like being a comfortable win for Harlequins as they dominated possession and territory in the first half, but they were wasteful in attack and Newcastle were tenacious in defence.

The competition again involved the 12 Aviva Premiership clubs plus the four Welsh sides from the Magners League. The format from 2009-10 was retained, with clubs playing against sides from another pool rather than those in their own.

Matches were played during the autumn internationals and RBS Six Nations, which meant that current internationals were usually unavailable, though England flanker Hendre Fourie appeared for Leeds Carnegie in their defeat at Northampton as a fitness test after he missed England's Six Nations opener in Cardiff with a calf strain.

The competition gave clubs an opportunity to blood some of their emerging academy stars, though Wasps were deducted a point after it was discovered that rookie back-row forward Joe Burton was not eligible to play for them in their defeat at newcomers Exeter. Wasps played Burton in the mistaken belief that he was dual-registered with National One club Rosslyn Park. The deduction made no difference to the placings in Pool One, which was won by Newcastle.

Northampton, the defending champions, failed to make it beyond the pool stage. For their opening cup matches they fielded a virtual second team, including Dan Sanderson, a lock/back-row forward, who was playing for Rolls-Royce at the bottom of the league pyramid 18 months earlier. Sanderson, spotted playing for Derby by Northampton's academy manager Alan Dickens, was offered trials at Franklin's Gardens while still working as a plasterer. He performed sufficiently well on his senior debut in the draw at Saracens to be offered a contract for the rest of the season, though he was released in May and joined Championship club Moseley.

Leicester, hard hit by injuries and international call-ups, also fielded a cup side that was barely recognisable compared with their regular Premiership XV and lost all four of their matches in Pool One. Harlequins were the only side to win all their pool matches, including a 34-25 win at Welford Road, their first victory over Leicester in 14 matches. They also edged out Newcastle 28-20 at the Twickenham Stoop, but the Falcons took their revenge four months later.

It proved to be a disappointing competition this year for the Welsh sides, with only the Dragons making it through the pool stage. They beat the Scarlets 26-9 at Rodney Parade to edge out Saracens, who knew they could not go any further before they hosted Sale at Vicarage Road later the same day. Mark McCall, the Saracens director of rugby, did not tell his players that they were out of the competition until after they had romped to 50-7 win in which Chris Wyles, the United States international winger, ran in a hat-trick of tries.

FACING PAGE Gloucester fly half Nicky Robinson gave a man-of-the-match display in the final, including a 14-point contribution from the boot. He has joined Wasps for 2011-12.

BELOW Saracens' James Short is surrounded by Regardt Dreyer, Dan Sanderson and Shane Geraghty of Northampton in the LV= Cup first-round clash at Vicarage Road, which ended in a 22-22 draw. Sanderson (second right) had enjoyed a meteoric rise into the big time.

PAGES **102-103** Celebration time for the Cherry and Whites.

Feel secure with us on your side

A range of protection products for people who live rugby every day

Talk to your financial adviser

LV= is proud to support Wooden Spoon

If you love it, LV= it

INSURANCE ♥ INVESTMENTS ♥ RETIREMENT

A Blip or a Trend?
the State of the Game in Wales
by GRAHAM CLUTTON

'Yes, the regions believe that a fruitless season is merely a blip in the greater scheme and of course three wins in five Six Nations games can be construed in any way that you wish'

It was hardly a season to remember for Welsh rugby. A disappointing autumn series, an equally frustrating Six Nations Championship and nothing to write home about in terms of the domestic game. In World Cup year, Welsh rugby finds itself in a period of transition.

Worrying? Well, of course. With players leaving to seek their fortune outside of the Principality and the Under 20s suffering so badly at the hands of New Zealand and Fiji in the Junior World Championship, there are genuine concerns about all areas of the game in Wales. Yes, the regions believe that a fruitless season is merely a blip in the greater scheme and of course three wins in five Six Nations games can be construed in any way that you wish. Unfortunately, for the ever-increasing number of critics who see Welsh rugby spiralling out of control, there is no such optimism.

Paul Turner, the former Dragons coach, said, 'With the way the game is developing in England and France and with the sums of money involved, I cannot see any one of our regions ever winning the Heineken Cup. We just can't compete.

'Yes, we have tried to stem the tide and keep in touch, but the fact that our players are beginning to leave tells you that there are bigger sums of money available elsewhere. I can't see that changing in the foreseeable future.'

Having already seen Dwayne Peel, Nicky Robinson, Andy Powell and Gareth Delve, amongst others, depart for pastures new, Welsh rugby will kick off World Cup season without the likes of Lee Byrne, Mike Phillips, Craig Mitchell and arguably the one shining light in an otherwise gloomy year, James Hook.

Kiwis Marty Holah and Jerry Collins have departed the Liberty Stadium, too, while Regan King and David Lyons have left Parc y Scarlets. These are certainly testing times for Welsh rugby's frontrunners, who have long been tipped as the genuine contenders to challenge for the ultimate prize. Sadly, silverware this season seems as unlikely as last, as the four cut their cloth accordingly.

The season began at a snail's pace, with a lack of success in the LV= Cup leading to only one of the four regions reaching the last four. However, by the time the Dragons pitched up at Kingsholm, to play Gloucester in the semi-final in March, the Cherry and Whites were on a decent run of form and duly eased into the final. 'Disappointing,' said coach Darren Edwards.

In the Heineken Cup, meanwhile, the Dragons were not alone when it came to underachieving. They finished bottom of Pool Six; the Ospreys, despite high hopes, finished third in Pool Three, behind Toulon and Munster; Cardiff Blues finished second in Pool One, but sadly missed out on qualification; the Scarlets suffered, too, ending up in third place, behind Perpignan and Leicester Tigers, in Pool Five. 'We are obviously gutted,' said Ospreys coach Sean Holley, whose side won three out of six pool games but finished two points behind Munster and a further point adrift of pool winners Toulon.

'Once again we have been competitive and have won half of our matches. But we were in a very tough group and find ourselves looking at next season. It's a great shame because I think we showed that we are one of the competition's leading teams.'

RESULT!

Our focus is helping our clients meet their goals.

We advise our clients on the planning and execution of strategies that generate the best results from the money they spend on their built assets. Our solutions are always tailored to client need and supported, by 100 years of technical professional skills and experience in the planning, creation, operation and utilisation of assets in the built environment.

**EC HARRIS
BUILT ASSET
CONSULTANCY**

TO FIND OUT HOW WE CAN HELP YOU GET THE BEST RESULT, VISIT US AT ECHARRIS.COM

They probably are, on paper. However, a lack of know-how and a plethora of mistakes in key games were to prove costly for all four sides. It was a European season to forget, with Welsh rugby, once again, back in the dock.

It was a similar story in the Magners League where the Ospreys once again led the way before missing out at the penultimate hurdle. Having won the grand final in 2010, the Welsh region finished the regular season in fourth place behind the Irish trio of Munster, Leinster and Ulster. A late surge from the Scarlets and Cardiff Blues suggested that possibly two sides would reach the play-off semi-finals, but in the end it was the Ospreys who edged into the top four for the second successive season.

Sadly, once again, it was to prove another bridge too far as Munster breezed into the final on the back of an 18-11 success against the Ospreys in Limerick. Richard Fussell bagged a second-half try for the Welsh region, but Munster were always in front and duly booked their place in the final, where they would eventually meet and beat Heineken Cup winners Leinster.

By the time the domestic season had been laid to rest, Welsh rugby was bracing itself for an all too familiar, damning post-mortem. Three victories in 10 matches, including the June international against the Barbarians, did little to appease the public who were, by now, reflecting on a season that had seen Welsh rugby fail to impose itself.

The autumn series was the perfect case in point, with three defeats and a near miss against Fiji confirming the underlying fears. Australia won 25-16 in early November and after South Africa had consigned Wales to a second successive defeat (29-25), Fiji snatched a 16-16 draw courtesy of a last-gasp penalty conceded by Wales captain Ryan Jones and converted by Seremaia Bai. The edgy nature of the Wales management was to raise its head in the after-match press conference when coach Warren Gatland, clearly disappointed by the penalty in the final minute, publicly stripped Jones of the skipper's armband.

The Scarlets hooker Matthew Rees took over in charge for the final game of the series, against New Zealand, but finished on the losing side. To their credit, Wales trailed by only five points, 23-18, with eight minutes remaining. However, 14 points in the closing moments for the tourists made the game safe, although Lee Byrne crossed for a consolation try late on. Wales lost 37-25 and Gatland, who saw Stephen Jones kick 20 points from six penalties and a conversion, said, 'We gave it a good go, but once again finished short.'

With injuries to, amongst others, Byrne, George North, Adam Jones, Gethin Jenkins and Shane Williams damaging preparations for the Six Nations, Wales went into the opening game of the championship, against England in Cardiff, in relatively poor shape. James Hook was once again asked to play out of position at full back, while Scarlets full back Morgan Stoddart found himself on the wing and Paul James and Craig Mitchell filled in for Jenkins and Jones respectively. England, too, had their difficulties, but on the night proved too strong for a Welsh side that defended poorly. Chris Ashton crossed the try line twice and man of the match Toby Flood kicked 13 points for good measure.

A comfortable 24-6 victory in Edinburgh was far and away the best performance of the championship by Wales, with Shane Williams touching down twice and Hook, back at outside half at last, adding 14 points with the boot.

Fuelled by renewed confidence but still short of their best, Wales managed to win in Rome two weeks later and followed up with a controversial victory over Ireland at the Millennium Stadium two weeks after that. A mix-up between the officials over a Welsh line out on halfway meant Mike Phillips was wrongly awarded a try that would enable Wales to hold off Ireland and register a third win in four games. Still, with England on a roll, Wales would need to win in France and rely on others to mess up to have any chance of challenging for the championship silverware.

It was not to be, and a 28-9 defeat in Paris just about summed up a season that saw Gatland's side finish in fourth place, albeit on the same points as France and Ireland. 'There have been some positive moments in the championship and some disappointments too,' said Gatland. 'However, we have to move on from here and make sure that when we get to New Zealand in September, we have learned some harsh lessons.'

Now all eyes are on New Zealand and on Wales's opening game of the World Cup against South Africa. Off-the-field problems surrounding Mike Phillips hardly helped the initial preparations, but Wales will head off with hopes and expectations high. Whether or not they can fulfil their dream remains to be seen. On the evidence of last season, I suggest that a quarter-final berth is the best they can hope for.

The Mighty Fallen
What Now for Wasps and Sale?

by **CHRIS FOY**

'There were similarities in how the last dismal campaign unfolded for the two clubs in that they both started out with coaches from New Zealand who were jettisoned along the way'

Wasps and Sale are two champion clubs with much in common despite the geographical gap between them. They have not always shared the closest of bonds in recent years, but what they have shared – sadly – is an emphatic decline. In Stockport to the north and High Wycombe to the south, these are teams who have lost their way after scaling the heights. They have made markedly different attempts to stop the rot, and this season will reveal which of the clubs, if either, is ready to rise again.

Wasps under Warren Gatland were Premiership champions three times in a row from 2003 to 2005, with a Heineken Cup triumph in 2004 and another three years later, during Sir Ian McGeechan's tenure, marking them out as a major force in domestic and European rugby. Sale's peak was more fleeting but provided a welcome break from the Leicester-Wasps duopoly when the

side coached by Philippe Saint-André claimed the league title in style, by finishing top of the table and going on to thrash Leicester 45-20 in a one-sided final.

The Sharks had finished third the year before their successful campaign and also won the European Challenge Cup for a second time by demolishing Pau 27-3 in the final. They went on to achieve respectable fifth-place Premiership finishes in 2008 and 2009, but the past two seasons have been all about survival, with the Cheshire club narrowly hanging on to their place in the elite on both occasions. In contrast, Wasps have been contenders until comparatively recently, but a fifth-place finish in 2010 was preceded by a disappointing seventh in 2009 and followed by last season's catastrophic slump to ninth.

There were similarities in how the last dismal campaign unfolded for the two clubs in that they both started out with coaches from New Zealand who were jettisoned along the way. At Sale, Mike Brewer's brief reign lasted just eight months. He was dismissed last December, having presided over a sequence of defeats, an overhaul of the playing staff and an ill-fated attempt to instil a hard-nosed Kiwi approach which only served to put noses out of joint all around him. He was sacked amid rumours of a player coup, although there was no dramatic up-turn in results under caretaker head coach and club stalwart Pete Anglesea.

At Wasps, Tony Hanks had been around since 2009, but he too paid for poor results as a further sign that rugby was adopting football's harsh, hiring-and-firing culture. Hanks had been a far more genial, popular figure than Brewer and someone with strong links to the club, having been an assistant coach before he stepped up to replace McGeechan, but there was a sense that he was not at home as the head of the operation. Leon Holden, another Kiwi, took over as director of rugby on an interim basis, but again this brought no miracle solution.

There have been other common themes in the downturn of these clubs and they are interlinked. First of all, both are stuck in inadequate grounds and are seeking enhanced homes. Wasps are aware of the limitations of Adams Park, at the end of an industrial estate, and their training facilities in Acton, west London, are famously archaic. Owner Steve Hayes has been trying to push through a move to a new, purpose-built stadium – to be shared with his other sporting interest, Wycombe Wanderers FC – in a far more suitable setting by the M40, but the whole project has been bogged down in the usual, endless cycle of planning meetings and protests and hold-ups. Meanwhile, Sale may have a more rapid solution, as they are considering the option of sharing a new ground with Salford City Reds rugby league club from next season. In the meantime, the Sharks players returned for pre-season to the welcome sight of a new, state-of-the-art training centre at their Carrington base.

Linked to the ground problem has been the fan problem. Both Wasps and Sale could count on full houses regularly when they were in their pomp, but the attendance figures have subsided in line with results. Both have tried to revive interest with bold ventures to Twickenham and Bolton's Reebok Stadium respectively, but without an immediate knock-on effect in terms of weekly headcount. They both hover around the 7000 mark as an average, which makes it difficult to compete with the likes of Northampton, who pull in 13,000-plus for every home game, and Leicester, who can count on crowds in excess of 20,000 at Welford Road.

That in turn has an impact on the financial predicament for both clubs. Sale owner Brian Kennedy had become disenchanted with the club's decline and repeatedly sought fresh investment to lessen the burden on his own finances. During the 2009-10 season, director of rugby Kingsley Jones and head coach Jason Robinson were forced to operate with a reduced budget that meant they were unable to recruit high-calibre players or even, in some cases, have access to vital equipment. At Wasps, there were rumours of unrest as club staffing levels were reduced and operations more closely linked with Wycombe Wanderers.

FACING PAGE Glory days for Wasps. Lawrence Dallaglio and comrades with the Heineken Cup after beating Leicester in the 2007 final.

BELOW Another great bows out. Phil Vickery (left), alongside Wasps' director of rugby Tony Hanks, announces his retirement from rugby in October 2010.

On the field, both clubs lost their sparkle with the departure of so many Galacticos. Crucially for Wasps, the retirement of Lawrence Dallaglio left a void that has been simply too big to fill. He was the captain, driving force and heartbeat of the team. James Haskell was identified as a successor, but then he left for Paris, to join Stade Français, along with Tom Palmer. Riki Flutey went to Brive and although he returned for last season, he was a pale imitation of the player who had won a Lions Test cap in 2009. Danny Cipriani fled to Melbourne and all of a sudden the team was lacking both international class and box-office appeal. Phil Vickery then retired and other stalwarts such as Simon Shaw and Joe Worsley were nearing the end of the line, with no sign of fitting replacements emerging. To have a journeyman such as Ben Jacobs leading Wasps last season – taking on Dallaglio's old role – showed the scale of the decline.

In terms of results, the fall from grace was highlighted by home-and-away humiliation at the hands of Northampton, with scores of 37-10 and 39-3 respectively. And yet, just before the end of the season, a huge home win over Leeds gave cause for some renewed hope, with the startling class of rookies such as Elliot Daly suggesting there could be better times ahead.

At Sale, the departure of Saint-André and the reduction in funds had brought an inevitable exodus. Out went the likes of Sébastien Chabal, Juan Martín Fernández Lobbe, Luke McAlister, Sébastien Bruno and Rory Lamont. They were not replaced in kind. Sure enough, the Sharks took their fair share of heavy beatings last season, going down 68-17 at Gloucester, 53-24 at Northampton and 54-21 at Leicester. However, they too had reason for hope in the emergence of talent through the academy, such as lock-cum-flanker James Gaskell and prop Henry Thomas.

The way the two clubs have responded to their demise has been markedly different. Wasps used Holden to see them through to the end of the season and also oversee player recruitment. The addition of England hooker Steve Thompson should add vital ballast and experience to a raw and often overpowered pack, but many of the new arrivals do not come with a proven pedigree. Holden was released at the end of last season and the search for a new director of rugby dragged on, with Dean Ryan rumoured to have turned down the role. Finally, at the end of June, Dai Young was brought in from Cardiff Blues, and capturing the respected former Wales and Lions prop represented a real coup. Yet, he will largely have to work with what he has been given for his first season, and he may soon realise that the squad lacks a depth of quality in many areas.

Sale's attempt to kick-start a revival was markedly more decisive and organised. Once Brewer had been sacked, ex-coach Steve Diamond was lined up for a return at the start of February, but even before he officially took up a new post as 'executive director of sport', he was busy doing what he does best – playing the transfer-market game. England prop Andrew Sheridan agreed to stay when he had been expected to leave and new recruits began signing in droves. With a total of 21 players being released, it was a root-and-branch overhaul of a failing squad. Diamond set about putting in place a formidable pack as the foundation of his new team, and that process came to a head with two key deals at the end of the season.

Once Leeds had been relegated, England's Afrikaner flanker, Hendre Fourie, was free to talk to other clubs, and despite interest from several, including London Irish, he agreed to join Sale. Yet, more pertinently in assessing the contrast between the Cheshire club and Wasps, Andy Powell departed from Wycombe under a cloud of controversy and soon pitched up in Stockport to join Diamond's revolution. The Wales No. 8 had been impressive in his first season at Wasps, but when he was embroiled in a fight with football fans in a west London pub, his employers investigated and chose not to offer him a new contract, despite supportive overtures from several team-mates. Seizing his chance, Diamond pounced to secure another player wanted by several clubs.

By no means can the departure of Powell from Wasps and his arrival at Sale alone signify that the former club will toil again this season and remain in a trough while the latter emerges as a contender once more – especially as he was destined to miss the start of the season while away at the World Cup with Wales. Yet, somehow, his move may come to symbolise a strong rebuilding of the former champions in the north, set against a continued weakening of the former champions in the south.

FACING PAGE Sébastien Chabal, former Sale talisman, in action for the Sharks against Montauban in the 2008-09 Heineken Cup.

BELOW A new generation. Sale's Henry Thomas runs into Will Skinner of Harlequins at The Stoop. Prop Thomas was a Junior World Championship finalist with England Under 20 in the summer.

It's rough out there

ParcourFM has developed a comprehensive FM service platform that will help you advance your game. We help our clients stay competitive in today's daunting economic market with flexible solutions to meet their specific project and FM needs. At a time when it's tougher than ever to be the lead player, it's even more critical to have the right strategy.

**It's a dirty job
but someone has to do it**

Interior Design, Furniture, Move Management, Warehousing, Logistics, Fit out, Refurbishment

parcourFM

Talk to us and see how we can help
www.parcourfm.co.uk
info@parcourfm.co.uk
t 01708 557 128

REVIEW OF THE SEASON 2010-11

Red Rose Revived
the 2011 Six Nations Championship
by CHRIS JONES

'It was a touch-line penalty just four minutes from time that elevated Bergamasco to hero status and signalled the start of a monumental party'

England were denied Grand Slam glory but still got to lift the Six Nations trophy for the first time in eight years amid chaotic – made for television – scenes in a Dublin hotel long after they had lost 24-8 to Ireland at the new Lansdowne Road stadium. With Wales having a slim chance of the title, the presentation had to wait until the late kick-off in Paris had finished, with the French triumphing 28-9 to allow the English players to, finally, uncork the champagne.

The limitations that were evident throughout England's campaign – most notably a midfield lacking the ability to open up a defence without using brute force – were exposed by the Irish, who celebrated Brian O'Driscoll's twenty-fifth championship try, which eclipsed Ian Smith in the record books. Equally important was Jonathan Sexton's performance. He has struggled to emerge from

Ronan O'Gara's shadow but kicked 14 crucial points to keep England on the back foot.

ABOVE Brian O'Driscoll scores for Ireland against England in Dublin. It was his twenty-fifth Six Nations try, taking him past Ian Smith's record of 24 in the Five/Six Nations.

FACING PAGE Chris Ashton swallow-dives in for the first of his four tries in England's 59-13 defeat of Italy at Twickenham.

The defeat took some of the gloss off England's championship, but Martin Johnson's men had come a long way during the Six Nations and discovered truly outstanding talents such as flanker Tom Wood and young prop Alex Corbisiero along the way, while Tom Palmer had emerged as a key line-out forward. There were also the headline-grabbing six-try swallow-diving antics of Chris Ashton to bring a smile to the faces of Red Rose fans, while scrum half Ben Youngs, full back Ben Foden and the kicking of Toby Flood all proved to be crucial during the bid for Slam glory that fell just short. However, at least they could head to the World Cup as northern hemisphere champions.

England's championship campaign started on a Friday night – yes, a FRIDAY night – in Cardiff, with Ashton bagging two tries and Flood kicking 13 points with calm assurance to keep the visitors out of reach of a Welsh side that saw Morgan Stoddart score their try and Stephen Jones chip in with 11 points. The English headed back over the Severn Bridge – the following morning – with a 26-19 win that had proved two things: England were capable of power rugby away from home and Friday night is hopeless if you are one of the thousands of Red Rose fans trying to get home from Wales when public transport has all but disappeared at that time of the night.

In Rome, Ireland were proving that they can be as infuriatingly inconsistent as their critics constantly claim. They messed around for 80 minutes before Ronan O'Gara broke Italian hearts with a last-gasp dropped goal that was good enough to earn a 13-11 win. It had looked so good for the home side after Luke McLean had dived over for a try that put them 11-10 ahead, only for Mirco Bergamasco, who would enjoy huge success and also massive disappointment with the boot, to miss the conversion. Martin Castrogiovanni had been Herculean in the scrums, but it was O'Gara – trying to prove he wasn't ready for the scrap heap – who came on as replacement for Jonathan Sexton to become Ireland's saviour yet again.

The French started what would become yet another championship of mixed performances by beating Scotland 34-21 to suggest – wrongly – that they could repeat the Six Nations triumph of a year ago. France had lost 59-16 to Australia in the autumn while Scotland were proving to be the most reliable of the Home Unions in the pre-Christmas Tests, and that Wallaby thrashing brought out the best in the French while the Scots seemed to have peaked too early in the season.

One of France's four tries came from their powerful scrum, which had Euan Murray in all kinds of trouble. The penalty try was inevitable as Murray was cruelly exposed by a French front row that was to be impressive throughout the campaign, and although the Scots fought back with tries from the hard-running Sean Lamont, skipper Alastair Kellock and Kelly Brown, they had too much ground to make up in Paris.

Italy failed to build on their good play against Ireland and collapsed in an ugly heap at Twickenham, where four-try Ashton dominated a 59-13 England win. His controversial swallow dive was on show, to the annoyance of Martin Johnson and the delight of the Twickenham faithful, who now had a new hero – one with individuality and a touch of madness. What other word could you use to describe someone who purposely went out to upset Johnson?

Ashton became the first player to score four tries in a championship match since the Six Nations was inaugurated in 2000 and equalled the individual record for a Six Nations season – six tries – held by Shane Williams and Will Greenwood. England racked up eight tries in total against Italy, with Flood kicking another 13 points and Jonny Wilkinson entering the fray to bang over three conversions and show off the tan he had picked up playing in the south of France with Toulon. The England players saved their longest celebration on the pitch for Mark Cueto's try, which ended an 18-Test drought for the popular left wing who must have been fed up clapping the six tries of Ashton in England's opening two championship matches. There was even a try for Mike Tindall – four years after his last one!

FACING PAGE Mike Tindall, World Cup winner in 2003 and captain of England in the 2011 Six Nations in the absence of Lewis Moody. More recently, he has become son-in-law to Wooden Spoon's Royal Patron.

BELOW Rome goes crazy! Italy have beaten reigning champions France for the first time in the Six Nations.

Scotland returned to Murrayfield and produced a dire showing as they lost 24-6 to Wales, who had Shane Williams to thank for two tries. The Welsh went down to 13 men at one stage, courtesy of two yellow cards, and all the Scots could muster was two Dan Parks penalties in the entire match. No wonder coach Andy Robinson had a face like thunder at the end of the contest.

The boot was on the other foot for Ireland as they conspired to score three tries to one and still lose 25-22 at home to France. Maxime Médard was on the try-scoring sheet again for the French, with Morgan Parra kicking five penalties and Dimitri Yachvili adding a critical penalty and conversion as Ireland coach Declan Kidney saw his side concede too many silly penalties. At the death, Ireland had one more chance to win the match, only for Sean Cronin to knock on with support outside him.

Morgan Stoddart and Sam Warburton scored pre-interval tries for Wales as they established a handy 21-11 first-half lead in Rome, with the Italians trying to bounce back from that heavy loss at Twickenham. The final score showed that Wales had held on for an unconvincing 24-16 win, losing the second half 5-3. It was another case of Italy throwing away a golden opportunity for a much-needed win to boost their confidence, and with Wales slotting a late dropped goal from the ever-dangerous James Hook it was tears before bedtime for coach Nick Mallett and his Italian forwards, who had once again produced a huge performance in the scrums.

England created just one try as they defeated reigning champions France 17-9, and it came from the always dangerous Ben Foden, who had been, like everyone else in the English back line, eclipsed by the heroics of Northampton clubmate Ashton. The English victory was marred by the loss to serious injury of prop Andrew Sheridan, although his replacement – London Irish rookie Alex Corbisiero – would produce amazingly mature performances in the rest of the championship. Yachvili kicked three penalties as France found England a much tougher proposition at Twickenham and had to accept second place in the contest that now set up the home side for a shot at the Grand Slam.

For Ireland, it was a case of back to the future for their trip to Murrayfield, and the evergreen O'Gara responded to his recall with a try as the Irish made it yet another reverse for Scotland, winning 21-18. All Scotland could muster was five penalties and a dropped goal, and this inability to finish off attacking moves was a weakness they could not overcome. Not even more examples of Irish indiscipline could help the home cause.

Just when we thought the Italians would have to endure another season of near misses, the penultimate round of matches threw up a 22-21 home win over France, the first time the Azzurri had knocked over Les Bleus in Rome. It sparked wild scenes of celebration, with many rugby fans outside Italy joining in to register their admiration for a country that had come so close this season to victories over Ireland and Wales. Morgan Parra and Vincent Clerc scored tries for France, but it was Mirco Bergamasco who kicked Italy to victory to experience unrestrained personal joy after so many bad days at the office. It was a touch-line penalty just four minutes from time that elevated him to hero status and signalled the start of a monumental party.

Ireland were not in party mood in Cardiff as a howler by the touch judge allowed Wales to win 19-13 after the home side took an illegal quick throw – using a different ball – and put Mike Phillips in for a try. With the excellent James Hook kicking 11 points, the Welsh were mathematically in with a chance of the championship title. Brian O'Driscoll had equalled Ian Smith's record with his twenty-fourth championship try, but that was clouded by the Phillips score, which showed that TV technology could have saved the officials from a storm of controversy if they had been able to call for a replay of the quick-throw incident.

England were expected to set up their Grand Slam decider with an easy win over the Scots but struggled to register a 22-16 triumph. Tom Croft returned after his shoulder injury to score the vital try, with Matt Banahan appearing as a second-half replacement at centre to add much-needed power in midfield. Max Evans scored an individual try for Scotland – a welcome visit to the in-goal area by a Scot in the championship – to have the Twickenham faithful biting their nails, but England held on for the win that sent them to Dublin in search of that Slam.

In the final round, Italy ended up with the Wooden Spoon as the Scots built on their improved showing at Twickenham with a 21-8 win. Italy were not helped by the loss of the impressive Andrea Masi – who scored their try – and Bergamasco was back to his unreliable self. Nick de Luca and Nikki Walker scored the Scottish tries to calm Robinson's frayed nerves. Paterson kicked 11 points and pulled off a brilliant, try-saving tackle on McLean to highlight his worth to the team.

For Wales, the maths didn't matter because their faint hopes of stopping England lifting the trophy were destroyed in Paris, with lock Lionel Nallet scoring two tries as the home side found some form to appease their many critics. Hook kicked the Welsh points, but they had come up short – much like the defending champions – at the end of a championship that was illuminated by Ashton's six tries and that win for Italy over France in Rome. Not a vintage year – but a thought-provoking way to head into the World Cup for everyone.

The Club Scene
England: The Clubs Still Provide
by TERRY COOPER

'For your next quiz night, try this on the know-all team. Name the clubs in the rejected prototype for National Leagues issued in 1981'

Not all the England World Cup summer training squad arrived in the national team via the southern hemisphere, school then a Premiership academy, or even through that baffling pastime they play in a couple of northern counties. The tradition lives on of lower-league clubs developing precocious talent and, seasons later, glowing with reflected pride when the local boy makes good in the white shirt.

One classic example is Tom Wood, whose route to Northampton and England included youthful years at Level 7 Midlands side Barkers' Butts. Bob Roberts, their secretary – no chief executives at that level – says, 'We look on him as one of ours. When he played for England he was our man. I don't think he appeared for anyone else before hitting the professional game.

'He has returned to us to do some coaching and participate in a Q&A. The kids idolise him. He was mobbed. He was like the Pied Piper. Of course, we have sent others to the top for masses of caps, notably Neil Back and Danny Grewcock.'

Rob Storey, secretary of West Park Leeds, in Level 8, expresses similar thoughts about ensuring that the younger players thrive. 'Danny Care was a mini with us when we were West Park Bramhope and we still feel that he belongs to us. One of the most important things that a club like ours can do is to ensure that all potential blossoms.' West Park swamp their area with up to a dozen sides most Saturdays, and their promotion last year was enhancing. 'We had a skip in our walk and a smile on our faces in the weeks of what was a stroll to promotion,' recalls Storey.

The huge league system that embraces 1200 clubs in about 120 divisions is even bigger than followers of the elite game suspect. Bob Roberts points out, 'Players want only leagues and we have competitive rugby for 2nd, 3rd and 4th teams. With the adult teams, vets, juniors, minis and women, over 200 people wear our shirt most weekends. Success is as blissful to us as the champions when they spray the champagne at Twickenham. When we were promoted we were euphoric.'

Among other England stars who emerged from relatively obscure origins are Courtney Lawes (Northampton Old Scouts until he was 16), Jonny Wilkinson (mini at Farnham), Tom Palmer (mini at Barnet Elizabethans), Andrew Sheridan (started at nine at Old Elthamians). It must be preferable for England's squad to comprise players from club sources rather than rugby league or overseas, whose provenance cannot be guaranteed.

For your next quiz night, try this on the know-all team. Name the clubs in the rejected prototype for National Leagues issued in 1981 – yes, 30 years ago. It was the brainchild of the great Eric Smith of Orrell. It was dismissed by the Rugby Union: 'Leagues, old boy? Can't have that. Too much like those soccer types.' Six years later, sanity cast a vote for change. But if Eric's proposal had been accepted in 1981, the first leagues would have lined up like this:

League One:	Bristol, Gloucester, Gosforth, Leicester, Moseley, Orrell, Rosslyn Park, Wasps, Waterloo.
League Two:	Bath, Bedford, Coventry, Fylde, Harlequins, Liverpool, London Irish, London Scottish, Richmond.

LEFT Northampton and England flanker Tom Wood, Aviva Premiership Player of the Season 2011, spent time at the Barkers' Butts club in Coventry before arriving in the top flight. Here he runs into opposition from Gloucester at Kingsholm.

League Three: Blackheath, Broughton Park, Exeter, London Welsh, Northampton, Nottingham, Roundhay, Sale, Wakefield.

No Worcester, obviously, or, indeed, current champions Saracens. When the union caved in to the trophy-seeking cads in 1987, Harlequins and Bath had managed to reach National Division One.

One highlight of the 2010-11 domestic club season was the prolonged series of rucks that Saracens withstood to beat Leicester in the Aviva Premiership play-off final. The Anglo-Welsh LV= Cup, meanwhile, stayed in English hands when Gloucester comfortably mastered Newcastle 34-7 in the final. The British & Irish Cup went to Bristol after their 17-14 success against Bedford.

Worcester returned to the Premiership by topping the Championship after the extensive play-offs. National League One was headed by London Scottish. The National Two Champions were Fylde (North) and Ealing Trailfinders (South), who earned their fifth promotion of the century. In the RFU knockout finals, Teddington claimed the Senior Vase, Stoke-on-Trent won the Intermediate Cup and HAC took the Junior Vase.

Lancashire again became county champions, appropriately winning the Bill Beaumont (Lancs to his core) Cup by overcoming Hertfordshire 32-23 in the final. The County Shield went to Dorset & Wilts and the Plate to Northumberland. The Middlesex Sevens title went to ULR Samurai International, an invitation specialist Sevens outfit, who beat holders London Irish 15-12 in the final.

The 33-day autumn bonanza of five big matches at Twickenham provided one of the true highlights in the game's history at HQ. It came early in the second half against Australia. After the Wallabies had been halted in the act of crossing England's line, the ball was audaciously slipped to wing Chris Ashton. He flew down the touch line, carved on an inside angle past the full back and completed his spectacular score with his now-trademark 'Ash Splash'. The ball travelled about 125 yards in just a few seconds – but still not as far as it did during Philippe Saint-André's try for France against England at Twickenham in 1991, when the ball changed direction three times while it sped 185 yards. It was Ashton's second, and Toby Flood contributed 25 points as Australia reeled from that freak try to go down 35-18. The All Blacks had won 26-16 a week earlier and then England saw off Samoa 26-13 before dipping 21-11 to the South Africans. But there was enough there to encourage manager Martin Johnson to have every confidence that his team could win the Six Nations for the first time since he held the trophy as captain in 2003. They obliged.

The Tests were followed by the Varsity Match, in which Oxford prevailed 21-10. The Wasps Academy centre Alex Cheesman scored one try and created another, thus ruining the day for Wasps coach Shaun Edwards, who helped with Cambridge's preparations for the big event.

Scotland: Premiership Closes the Gap by ALAN LORIMER

'There is a sense among the top four clubs of a determination to narrow the gap between the amateur and professional layers of rugby in Scotland'

For fans of professional club rugby in Scotland, the final placings in the Magners League together with results in the Heineken Cup provided little cheer. Edinburgh were eighth in the Magners League table and Glasgow eleventh, one place above the bottom club, Aironi, while in European rugby, both the Scottish participants were effectively beached after the first three rounds.

Yet all is not as gloomy as it might seem. Success in professional club rugby is for the most part determined by levels of investment, and quite simply Scotland's two clubs are near the bottom when it comes to the stash of hard cash being pumped in. But if the Magners League table were recalibrated using a weighting factor that took into account investment levels, then a different interpretation might emerge. Which is why it was slightly puzzling that the purse-string bosses at

Murrayfield took the decision to sack Edinburgh's coach, Rob Moffat, a move that surely left Glasgow coach Sean Lineen feeling less than secure in his own tenure. Lineen, however, could plead in mitigation the absence through injury of Chris Cusiter and Johnnie Beattie and the loss of Dan Parks to Cardiff.

Without the money to hire ex-All Blacks or Springboks or indeed Samoans, each of the two Scottish clubs was doomed to struggle in a league of bigger spenders. It's a situation that has been tacitly accepted by fans north of the border, who know that success in the Magners League or in Europe will be elusive as long as Murrayfield maintains a strict control on budgets for the professional clubs.

So what is the point of the Scottish professional clubs? The answer is that they provide the conduit through which potential international players can reach their goal – and perhaps quicker than in clubs crammed with foreign imports.

And that is certainly the case at both Edinburgh and Glasgow, the east coast club last season having undoubtedly accelerated the career

LEFT Edinburgh's Dutch wing Tim Visser celebrates with Scott MacLeod (No. 4) after scoring the winning try in his side's 23-16 Magners League victory over the Ospreys at Murrayfield.

FACING PAGE Richie Gray secures the restart as Glasgow Warriors defeat Wasps 20-10 in the Heineken Cup at Firhill.

of Greig Laidlaw, who solved Edinburgh's problems at fly half after understudying Mike Blair in the scrum-half berth, as well as that of David Denton, the abrasive back-row who made stunning progress in the second half of the season. At Glasgow, back-row Rob Harley and prop Ryan Grant were selected for the preliminary World Cup squad, teenager Duncan Weir launched his challenge for the Scotland fly-half position, and youngsters like full back Stuart Hogg and centre Peter Horne were given early opportunities to prove their worth.

Edinburgh may have lacked a forward pack with 'grunt', but that did not prevent their eight from providing enough possession for Tim Visser to show his exciting skills as a try-scoring winger, and for James King to demonstrate his talents as an inside centre.

If overall success was not evident at Edinburgh, then there were at least some uplifting wins, notably the Magners League victories at Murrayfield against Ulster and the Ospreys. In Europe Edinburgh fans felt the frustration of defeats in the first three pool matches by a total margin of ten points before their club finally achieved a result with a home win over Castres. But a bottom-place finish in the group summed up the grim situation and almost certainly sounded the death knell for Moffat.

Fifty miles to the west, Glasgow performed much better in Europe, with two wins over the Dragons and a victory against Wasps to finish third in their group – insufficient, though, for a quarter-final place. If Europe had provided some hope for Glasgow, then their Magners League results must have extinguished it, Glasgow finishing the season with only six wins.

In the absence of Johnnie Beattie, Richie Vernon grabbed the chance to stake his claim to a Scotland back-row place, while Richie Gray continued to excite with a series of exhilarating performances that made him a racing certainty for the lock position in the Scotland pack. Glasgow, however, simply lacked the back-up players to perform when their front-line troops were away, Lineen frequently bemoaning how difficult it was for inexperienced players 'to compete against tried and tested performers'.

Murrayfield's signal that no further money could be put into the professional clubs had, so some conspiracy theorists think, the intended result of forcing Scotland international players to move south. First on the move was Vernon, who snapped up an offer from Sale. The Manchester outfit also bid successfully for Edinburgh's exciting back-five player Fraser McKenzie. Max Evans was another to take his talents out of Scotland, the centre-cum-wing opting to play his rugby in France, while Edinburgh and Scotland lock Scott MacLeod took the route more associated with New Zealanders, by heading to Japan.

If this talent drain continues, Scotland could find itself mirroring the situation that until recently prevailed in Argentina, where the Puma players were all contracted to European clubs. That would kill off any hopes of league or cup successes, but the gaps created by migration south could offer opportunities for a new stream of players to experience professional rugby. And that might include more players from the top layer of amateur club rugby moving into the professional game. Hitherto professional rugby had been cautious about recruiting older players from the amateur game, but last season the performances of three clubs, Melrose, Ayr and Currie, in the British & Irish Cup altered the view from the professional bridge.

Melrose skipper and fly half Scott Wight broke the mould after being offered a contract with Glasgow at the end of a season in which the 25-year-old Melrosian steered his club to victory in the Scottish Premiership, the Border League and the Kings of the Sevens competition, as well as playing for the Scotland Club International side against Ireland and France.

It was a first league title for Melrose since 1997, when their current coach, Craig Chalmers, was one of several Scotland players in the victorious Greenyards side. Fourteen seasons later, Melrose played delightfully open rugby to win the championship in style ahead of second-placed Currie, with Ayr in third place in the final Premier A table. Ayr, however, ensured that Melrose would not monopolise all the trophies on offer by defeating them in the cup final at Murrayfield.

But what marked out the top three as teams narrowing the gap between the amateur and professional games was their performances, albeit inconsistent, in the British & Irish Cup. Melrose defeated Esher before giving Bristol a fright by running the West Country club close in a 26-29 defeat. Currie, too, posted good displays in defeats by Cornish Pirates, Newport and Plymouth Albion, but it was Ayr who did Scottish rugby proud by finishing second in their pool with three wins and one draw to secure a place in the quarter-finals.

It was not only Scott Wight who attracted interest from the professional ranks. Melrose wing-cum-full back Fraser Thomson was also offered a contract, but south of the border at Sale. Currie's fly half, Matthew Scott, too has cashed in after an impressive season at Malleny Park to become part of the Edinburgh set-up.

Just behind the top three league clubs were Glasgow Hawks, who under the direction of former Scotland and Lions prop Peter Wright were serious challengers for

RIGHT Ayr's Scotland Under 20 centre Mark Bennett evades Melrose scrum half Rob Chrystie on his way to the line in the cup final, which Ayr won 25-21 to prevent a Melrose league and cup double. Bennett left Ayr in the summer to join Clermont Auvergne.

championship honours. Hawks certainly have talented players, the pick of the crop from last season being their strong-running centre Dean Kelbrick, another to come under the gaze of professional eyes.

With little sign of increased investment in Edinburgh and Glasgow, there is a sense among the top four clubs of a determination to narrow the gap between the amateur and professional layers of rugby in Scotland. Certainly the standard of rugby in the top division of the Premiership was the highest it has ever been, and there are signs of a greater degree of 'professionalism' within the top teams.

The challenge will be establishing that approach further down the Premiership, but whether clubs like Heriot's, Boroughmuir, Dundee, Hawick and Aberdeen have the will, the drive and the resources to follow the leaders remains to be seen.

Elsewhere in the Premiership, Selkirk lost their fight to avoid relegation, along with Watsonians, their places in the top flight being taken by Stirling County and Gala, both of whom will add colour to a Premiership regarded by many as the most watchable club rugby in Scotland.

Ultimately the professional clubs depend on amateur clubs to produce the players of the future, but in the coming years it may be that the nursery products stay with what could be a new group of pro teams free of Murrayfield control. And the 2010-11 club season certainly gave hints that such an outcome may yet happen and not simply remain in the realms of fantasy rugby.

Wales: Last Season In Reverse

by DAVID STEWART

'The Ospreys' Welsh internationals played till the autumn Tests, went away for a month, came back for the Heineken and then disappeared for the Six Nations'

A season of progress if you were a Dragons or Scarlets fan. For followers of the Blues and particularly the Ospreys, it was a different story. There is an odd symmetry in that verdict. A year earlier we were reporting good seasons for the Swansea-Neath and Cardiff-Rhondda regions, while hinting at a bleaker future for those to the western and eastern ends of the south Wales coastline.

A wider view shows a Magners League table that is becoming stratified. Irish provinces occupied the top three slots, with Munster coming top of the table and going on to win the grand final; the Welsh regions filled fourth to seventh places in the table; the 'also-rans' made up the bottom tier. Organisers (and sponsors) will hope it is not the shape of things to come.

The reasons for the revivals in the Llanelli and Newport regions have similar roots: a predominantly youthful squad, supplemented by some committed and wise 'old heads', eager and

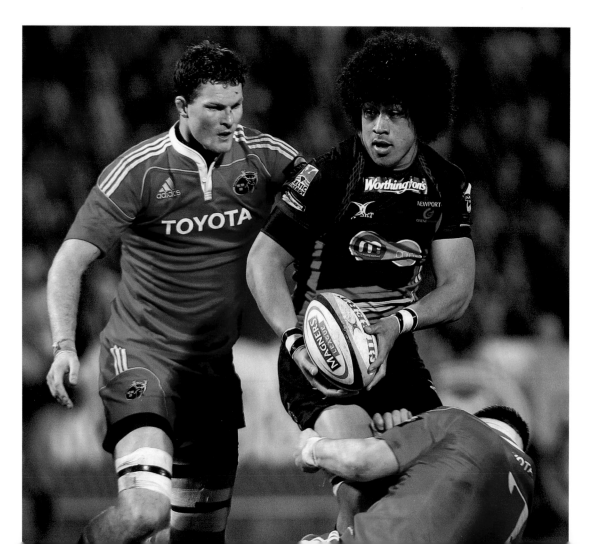

innovative coaching, and an expansive game plan. For the likes of Matthew Rees and Iestyn Thomas at the Scarlets, read Luke Charteris and Gavin Thomas in Gwent. For Nigel Davies setting the tone at Parc y Scarlets, read Darren Edwards at Rodney Parade. Edwards, a former Saracens and Newport scrum half, took over mid-season from Paul Turner, the latter departing in unhappy circumstances, having made a strong contribution to the region's survival as a competitive force, with an impressive home record.

Such was the progress of local youngsters, some overseas players eventually took a back seat – Scarlets No. 8 Ben Morgan (of whom great things are expected, but in an English or Welsh shirt?) and Dragons hooker Lloyd Burns kept David Lyons and Tom Willis on the bench in the latter part of the season.

It is often easier to catch the eye of representative selectors in a team going well. Self-evident then that – in addition to the established Dan Lydiate – Dragons Charteris, Burns, Toby Faletau (of Tongan extraction) and Aled Brew were all named by Warren Gatland at one point or another towards the season's end; not so many made full Welsh squads a year earlier.

Highlights of the Dragons' season included 'doing the double' over the Ospreys by the close margins of 21-16 in October and 32-28 in April; beating Munster (albeit shorn of their Irish squad players) 20-6 at home in November; and defeating old rivals the Blues 28-15 in April, that result effectively depriving the Cardiff region of a place in the play-offs. To top off the season, Brew and Faletau were named Player and Young Player of the Year respectively at the Welsh Rugby Players' Association (WRPA) awards. Much-needed redevelopment of the Dragons' ground, including a new Bisley Stand, leads to an air of optimism for the season ahead.

Effective leadership was another common factor at the Dragons and the Scarlets. A new captain of region and nation, Matthew Rees was a revelation. His example, allied to a fast and seemingly fearless style under the direction of Nigel Davies, saw the Scarlets revert to the type of rugby with which the west Walians have so long been associated. They missed the play-offs by the narrowest of margins, leading Davies to observe, 'People say we are two or three players short of being a top

ABOVE Aled Brew races in to score for the Dragons in their 28-15 Magners League victory over the Blues in April.

FACING PAGE WRPA Young Player of the Year Toby Faletau of the Dragons looks around for support as he is tackled by Donnacha Ryan and James Coughlan (No. 7) of Munster in the Magners League clash at Musgrave Park, Cork, in March. Munster won this one 38-17.

team, but you can't tell me this group haven't been good enough. We've just lost a couple of key moments in games which have made the difference.'

Robert Jones, once on the Scarlets' coaching staff, agreed. 'They have provided the best performances of any Welsh team in the Magners by some distance. They entertain, they go out and throw the ball around, they play to their strengths. They are an 80-minute side as well. Overall they have been a real success story.'

Stephen Jones, Morgan Stoddart, Jon Davies, George North (his progress in the next few seasons will fascinate), Scott Williams, Lou Reed, Josh Turnbull, Rhys Priestland and Tavis Knoyle make an impressive list of Scarlets who attracted national selection attention. The region's most popular wins were the 38-23 victory over the Blues in early May, on top of the earlier 16-10 triumph in Cardiff back in October.

Passing judgment on the two more powerful regions, Kingsley Jones, the former Sale director of rugby, said, 'We expect the Blues and Ospreys to deliver all the time, but the Blues depend heavily on a few senior players – like Xavier Rush – hitting their straps.'

Indeed. Warming to his theme, Jones went on. 'Their set-pieces struggled towards the end of their season, key players seemed to run out of steam. Their line out has been a blip but Paul Tito is a fantastic organiser. With no extra budget for new signings, they have to look at younger players to bring fresh impetus and keep those senior players on their toes.'

Dai Young, honest as always, summed up the Blues' plight after they had lost their final league games 38-23 to the Scarlets and 28-15 to the Dragons. 'We have to be honest and say for this season, it hasn't quite happened for us. Ball in hand, we've been found wanting. The stats don't lie, we've only scored 33 tries. What we've got to do is dust ourselves off, go back, and work on it.'

And then, having surveyed his options, the head coach accepted an offer to head east up the M4 and take over at Wasps. The new season will see the Cardiff region in the hands of Gareth Baber and Justin Burnell, who have been on the staff for several seasons; one anticipates these are 'holding' appointments till after the World Cup.

While the Blues have talented outside backs aplenty – Jamie Roberts, Chris Czekaj, Leigh Halfpenny, Tom James, and Richard

LEFT The Scarlets play a 'fast and seemingly fearless style' of rugby under their head coach, former Wales centre Nigel Davies.

FACING PAGE Ospreys scrum half Rhys Webb makes a break against the Blues in their 2010-11 LV= Cup tie at Cardiff City Stadium.

Mustoe – Jones hit on a key problem. 'They haven't been creative enough behind, in terms of imagination and the way they play. Dan Parks is part of that. I do feel No. 10, a key position, needs to be addressed.'

The Ospreys, meanwhile, had to win their last league game at Aironi to make the play-offs. That they succeeded 12-10 by means of a last-minute James Hook penalty – courtesy of a home forward with a loose lip – was a metaphor for their misfiring season, with a team that performed like a racing engine which needs stripping down and reassembling.

Good job therefore that several of the so-called marquee names (Lee Byrne, Mike Phillips, Hook) opted for pastures new, French ones. This kick-started the retooling work that was so obviously required from elite performance director Andrew Hore and his fellow Antipodean Scott Johnson.

Interestingly, the duo made clear that a lack of consistency in player availability was a contributory factor in the region's inconsistent results. Their Welsh internationals played till the autumn Tests, went away for a month, came back for the Heineken and then disappeared for the Six Nations. Thus the run-on XV acquired different personae – and team spirit – depending on the stage of the season. This has intriguing implications for those responsible for running the national XV.

Talent is not an issue, particularly in the front row, with Ryan Bevington, Paul James and Adam Jones making up a trio of props that persuaded Welsh Six Nations tight-head Craig Mitchell to move on. Tom Prydie will be available again after injury and scrum half Rhys Webb has terrific potential.

The Heineken Cup makes only a fleeting appearance in this narrative. For good reason – no regional team made the knockout stage, and for a proud (albeit not wealthy) rugby country, that is not good enough.

Wooden Spoon
The children's charity of rugby

BEHIND SCOTTISH RUGBY.

THE
**FAMOUS
GROUSE**
SCOTLAND'S FAVOURITE
WHISKY

Ireland: Rugby Atop a Pedestal

by SEAN DIFFLEY

'Just a week after the triumph in Cardiff, Leinster had another appointment to fulfil, the Magners League final against their perennial rivals, Munster'

No Grand Slam, no Triple Crown for Ireland, but in a general post-mortem of the past season, there is every justification in labelling it the most productive period ever in Irish rugby. An island of just five million population, with rugby as a domestic sport occupying a notch well below Gaelic games and soccer, now stands on a pedestal that looms the highest in the game in the northern hemisphere. Perhaps the most telling statistic is that all four Irish clubs, or provinces – Leinster, Munster, Ulster and, for the first time, Connacht – will take part in next season's Heineken Cup. Connacht, that lonely outpost on the far west, has from time immemorial been dubbed the 'Cinderella' province, and it is not that long ago that a protest march was held on Lansdowne Road amidst rumours that the Irish Rugby Football Union, concerned about financial considerations, were about to disaffiliate Connacht. But they didn't and instead a professional staff has been installed and there are plans now to erect a second stand on the Galway Sportsground. Much credit for Connacht's advance, through improvements in the Magners League and Amlin Challenge Cup, goes to their coach, Eric Elwood. In his playing days for Lansdowne, Connacht and Ireland, Elwood was an out-half, and his two penalty goals and the conversion of Simon Geoghegan's memorable try gave Ireland a 13-12 win at Twickenham in 1994.

But, of course, the major success of last season was Leinster's winning back of the Heineken Cup in Cardiff, where there was that extraordinary 33-22 win in the final over Northampton, despite being behind 22-6 at half-time and appearing to be destined for a total banjaxing. Whatever happened in the Leinster dressing room at the interval – Jonny Sexton is said to have forcibly reminded his team-mates of Liverpool's famous three-goal recovery – it worked like the magic of Merlin. Northampton failed to score in that second half, and the only comparable fightback was the French revival against the All Blacks in the 1999 World Cup semi-final at Twickenham when they gobsmacked the Jonah Lomu-inspired New Zealanders and turned a deficit of 10-24 into a sensational 43-31 victory.

All of which shows that nothing can be taken for granted in sport (betted on any horses recently?). That second-half performance by Leinster was greeted with deserving praise from all quarters, neutral observers judging it one of the greatest team

RIGHT Connacht head coach and former Ireland stand-off Eric Elwood watches the Ulster Bank Division 1B match between Galwegians and Lansdowne at Crowley Park in February.

displays ever. It was, of course, a particular triumph for 25-year-old fly half Jonny Sexton, the man of the match, who contributed an incredible 28 points in the match – two tries, three conversions and four penalty goals. Scotland lock Nathan Hines, who crossed for the third try, was the only other Leinster scorer, and he, with Leinster captain and fellow lock Leo Cullen, contributed so influentially to the win.

It was no easy path to eventual triumph. In their nine Heineken Cup matches, Leinster lost only one, a 13-20 reverse to Clermont Auvergne, but even then they gained a valuable losing bonus point and went on to win 24-8 in the return a week later in Dublin. The other wins were over Racing Métro 92 (38-22 and 36-11), Saracens (25-23 and 43-20), Leicester (17-10) and reigning champions Toulouse (32-23). That semi-final had a remarkable start: David Skrela's penalty came back into play after hitting a post, Florian Fritz catching the ball to score the easiest of tries. But Leinster soldiered on successfully, maintained their composure as Brian O'Driscoll scampered over for a typical try and duly qualified for their second Heineken Cup final in three years.

Just a week after the triumph in Cardiff, Leinster had another appointment to fulfil, the Magners League final for the Celtic championship – and that at Thomond Park against their perennial rivals, Munster, hitherto the Irish stars in the European Cup. The competitive spirit between those two leading Irish teams is pretty intense and the stadium and its red-jerseyed supporters plus a fair few blue-clad Leinster fans made that very clear. Munster finished 13 points clear of Leinster at the top of the league table and were determined to show that even if their season had been below their usual standards, Leinster of all people were not going to lord it over them. As it turned out, Leinster looked listless and well below form, and Munster demonstrated that they are far from a spent force, some like Ronan O'Gara making it clear that youngsters like Sexton weren't quite in the driving seat yet.

A very graphic illustration of Munster's superiority and Leinster's hangover after the Heineken triumph came late in the game when in a classic coup de grâce – or as the dictionary has it 'a blow delivered as an act of mercy to a sufferer' – the Munster set scrum powered Leinster back on their own line and referee Nigel Owens immediately blew his whistle and awarded Munster a penalty try. O'Gara's simple conversion was like the final act of a theatrical drama, with the curtain coming

down with an applauded flourish on Munster's 19-9 victory. So, the questions arise. What happened to Leinster the highly praised European champions? Were they suffering from the short period allowed since the Cardiff triumph? Were two finals in a week too much stamina-wise? And it all added further to the questions, too, about Northampton's collapse in the second half of the Heineken final. Frankly, tiredness cannot be tolerated as an excuse. Remember, most of the players will participate in the World Cup and most of the matches will be played within six or seven days of one another.

On a lower plane, in the All Ireland League (now sponsored by Ulster Bank) the 2011 winners were Old Belvedere, ousting the Munster club sides which usually dominate at this level. Belvedere, the home club of such stars of the game as Tony O'Reilly and Ollie Campbell, returned to the AIB first division for the 2007-08 season, and last year saw off Clontarf 22-20 in the semis before defeating Cork Constitution 20-17 in the final at Donnybrook to lift the first division title for the first time.

LEFT Referee Nigel Owens signals the award of a penalty try against Leinster as Munster beat the Heineken Cup holders to win the Magners League grand final.

ABOVE Old Belvedere celebrate with the Ulster Bank Division 1 trophy.

next

We are proud to support **The Wooden Spoon Rugby World**

www.next.co.uk

France: Novès Makes the Difference

by CHRIS THAU

'Bézy took the penalties with calm, as if there were no pressure to handle, the first to help Toulouse nudge ahead 12-10, and then the second to win the match 15-10'

The presence of Montpellier for the first time ever in the final of the French Championship at Stade de France gave the 110th Bouclier de Brennus clash an air of novelty, though it was a kind of déjà vu for veteran finalists Toulouse on their twenty-fifth appearance. Toulouse had finished the home-and-away section of the league at the top with 82 points, with Racing Métro as runners-up with 78 points and Castres third with 76 points; the trio of Clermont, Biarritz and Montpellier followed with 72 points each.

BELOW Montpellier players rush to congratulate Argentinian centre Santiago Fernández, who has just scored against Racing Métro to help put his side in the Top 14 final for the first time.

Montpellier had managed to make it into the top six thanks to a remarkable 27-3 demolition of star-studded Toulon in the last round of the home-and-away stage of the league. That win, described by Montpellier coach Fabien Galthié as 'a perfect match', took the club into the knockout phase of the league, at the expense of Toulon, who finished eighth. The momentum of that victory carried Montpellier on to the final, with successive one-point defeats of Castres (18-17) away and Racing Métro (26-25) in a breath-taking Marseille semi-final, while Toulouse confirmed their billing as the leading contender by putting the previous year's champions Clermont Auvergne to the sword 29-6 in the semis, also in Marseille.

The return of Stade Toulousain to the top of the French rugby hierarchy was predictable. They are after all the biggest club in the French game, thanks to their large supporter base and the business operation run by president René Bouscatel. But it is not only money that gives them the edge. Based on their salary bill alone, their rivals Toulon, very much the rugby equivalent of the United Nations, should stay at the top of French rugby in perpetuity. Nor is it the training facilities, nor their player base. Virtually all 14 clubs of the French premier league and even some of the top Pro D2 (professional division two) clubs spend the same amount of time training and with similar intensity, eat the same food, watch the same DVDs, lift the same weights, listen to the same match analysis – yet somehow Toulouse seem to reach the top with monotonous regularity. The unanimous conclusion of the French pundits in the aftermath of a passionate encounter in the final was that all being equal, it is the Toulouse coach, or director of rugby, Guy Novès, that makes the difference.

Although for 70 long minutes of the match it looked as if Galthié and his team were going to steal the show, the patience and sangfroid of Novès and his coaching team of Yannick Bru and Jean-Baptiste Elissalde paid off as young Nicolas Bézy, the replacement outside half, landed two vital penalties – all this after David Skrela's nightmarish afternoon, during which he missed no less than five kicks at goal.

Bézy took the penalties with calm, as if there were no pressure to handle, the first to help Toulouse nudge ahead 12-10 in the 71st minute, the first time Toulouse had found themselves in the driving seat, and then the second in the 75th minute to win the match 15-10. Novès had won again – it was the eleventh Bouclier de Brennus of his career, nine times as coach and two as a player, and all of them for and with Toulouse. Talk about records!

Guy Novès is intense yet thoughtful and has a rare capacity to rejuvenate himself and the team. He has got a keen eye for detail and a unique scouting ability. A good example of his uncanny ability to identify talent was the way the Toulouse wizard picked a newly signed scrum half, 20-year-old Jean-Marc Doussain, to start in the final, although he had only 18 matches as a professional player under his belt. Needless to say, Doussain had an absolute blinder.

Meanwhile, at the bottom end of the Top 14, both La Rochelle and Bourgoin have packed their bags for Pro D2, while Lyon and Bordeaux are coming up. Further down, St Etienne and Colomiers have been relegated to the division below, currently named Fédérale 1, with old campaigners Béziers and Périgueux winning promotion to Pro D2.

On the international front, it was enough for France to lose to Italy in the Six Nations for the knives to come out for French coach Marc Lièvremont. At the beginning of May, the prestigious *Midi Olympique* magazine was lamenting the state of the French game under the depressing title 'The big mess of French rugby'. What have we done during the 16 years since the game turned professional? asked *Midi Olympique* rhetorically. 'France has won five new Grand Slams in 1997, 1998, 2002, 2004 and 2010, but never the Webb Ellis trophy, while Argentina, Australia and South Africa have defeated France with record scores. And this is without mentioning the first defeat in the Six Nations at the hands of Italy. France is only 6th in the IRB rankings, behind the three Southern Hemisphere giants and the duo England and Ireland.'

This seems mildly unreal, at a time when the game in France is thriving. However, this is the ritual media bash before an RWC tournament, when everything from playing personnel to coaches and from administration to facilities comes under scrutiny. However, should France reach the final of the RWC in New Zealand, which is by no means an impossibility, I believe all will be forgiven.

Italy: Petrarca Win After 29 Years
by **CHRIS THAU**

'Rovigo surged ahead through two tries, only for Petrarca Padova to fight back with two tries from their live-wire hooker Agustín Costa Repetto'

There is no doubt that Italian rugby has benefited from the inclusion of Treviso and Aironi in the Magners League, as the past season has proved. This was very much the dream of former national coach Georges Coste, the Frenchman who took Italy to a position of respectability in the world of rugby during the mid- and late 1990s. He believed, rightly, that by providing Italian teams with a consistently high standard of opposition, the quality of the domestically based players would improve.

This is what has been happening with Treviso, the Rolls-Royce of Italian rugby, who bagged nine league wins, a win rate of nearly 50 per cent, beating some of the leading European sides, including Leinster, Munster and the Scarlets, as well as the other Italian Magners League entry, Aironi. The latter played reasonably good rugby at times, but they failed to ignite when it mattered and finished last in the table with only one win, which led to the departure of their long-serving coach Franco Bernini, who was replaced by former Wales back-row man Rowland Phillips. Despite that, the 100-odd contracted players of both Aironi and Treviso were exposed to elevated levels of rugby throughout the season, which was reflected in the performance of the Italian team, who had one of their better seasons since joining the Six Nations in 2000. One aspect that remains open to debate is whether the pace of improvement is high enough to advance Italy to a lead position in European and world rugby.

On the other hand, the exit of both Treviso and Aironi from the leading domestic competition, the Campionato Nazionale Eccellenza (Super 10), definitely lowered the standard of the championship. At the end of the league season, Rovigo dominated the table with 73 points, followed by I Cavalieri Prato with 67, Petrarca Padova with 59 and Crociati with 48. Venezia Mestre, who finished last, were relegated, with former first division regulars Calvisano winning promotion. Meanwhile, Rugby Roma Olimpic defeated Mogliano 33-12 in the final of the Italian knockout cup competition at Prato.

In the Super 10 home-and-away play-offs, Rovigo had the better of Crociati 20-13 and 24-9, while Petrarca Padova beat I Cavalieri Prato 31-18 and 6-5. The final between two former champions of Italy saw Petrarca Padova, coached by Pasquale Presutti, win 18-14 against a resolute Rovigo side coached by South African Polla Roux. Rovigo surged ahead through two tries scored by Luke Mahoney and Andrea Bacchetti, both converted by outside half German Bustos, only for Petrarca Padova to fight back with two tries from their live-wire hooker Agustín Costa Repetto. Full back Ludovic Mercier added a conversion and two penalties to secure Padova the title after a 29-year wait. This was Petrarca's twelfth championship title, the first of which was won in 1970.

Italy's narrow 22-21 win against France could well be regarded as their best result of the season, though the 11-13 defeat at the hands of

Ireland was perhaps Italy's most confident Six Nations performance in recent years. After losing 13 matches in a row between November 2008 and November 2009, Italy managed to beat Samoa, Fiji and Scotland, bringing a desperately poor sequence to an end, while saving Nick Mallett's job as well. Yet, despite considerable progress in most areas of play the Italian potential has yet to be fully and consistently harnessed.

This is not Nick Mallett's fault, though local critics argue that he has done precious little to alter Italy's one-dimensional pattern, based on the force of the scrum. This might be unfair criticism, taking into account that it was one of Italy's backs, the talented Andrea Masi, who was voted the player of the 2011 Six Nations Championship. However, in the end, despite the satisfying defeat of France, Mallett was told that his contract with the Azzurri would end after the RWC in New Zealand, no matter whether Italy reached the knockout stages (for the first time ever) or not.

It is said that the relationship between Mallett and Italian federation president Giancarlo Dondi deteriorated dramatically after the Wales match in the Six Nations, when Mallett was alleged to have left his table, for whatever reason, during Dondi's post-match speech. On the other hand, all this might be just coincidental speculation, as Italian pundits point out that Mallett was never the frontrunner for the Italian job, having been appointed when Dondi was told that the man initially approached, Frenchman Jacques Brunel, had already signed a contract with Perpignan. Brunel has eventually agreed terms to join Italy after the World Cup, which returns Italy to the French coaching school, amply represented in the past by leading professionals of the likes of Pierre Villepreux, Bertrand Fourcade, Georges Coste and Pierre Berbizier.

BELOW Petrarca Padova celebrate their first Italian Championship title for 29 years. Man of the match Agustín Costa Repetto, towards the right of the picture, holds the trophy in his right hand.

A Summary of the Season 2010-11

by TERRY COOPER

INTERNATIONAL RUGBY

AUSTRALIA TO EUROPE
NOVEMBER 2010

Opponents	Results
Wales	W 25-16
Leicester	W 26-15
England	L 18-35
Munster	L 6-15
Italy	W 32-14
France	W 59-16

Played 6 Won 4 Lost 2

NEW ZEALAND TO UK & IRELAND
NOVEMBER 2010

Opponents	Results
England	W 26-16
Scotland	W 49-3
Ireland	W 38-18
Wales	W 37-25

Played 4 Won 4

SOUTH AFRICA TO UK & IRELAND
NOVEMBER 2010

Opponents	Results
Ireland	W 23-21
Wales	W 29-25
Scotland	L 17-21
England	W 21-11
Barbarians	L 20-26

Played 5 Won 3 Lost 2

SAMOA TO UK & IRELAND
NOVEMBER 2010

Opponents	Results
Ireland	L 10-20
England	L 13-26
Scotland	L 16-19

Played 3 Lost 3

FIJI TO EUROPE
NOVEMBER 2010

Opponents	Results
France	L 12-34
Wales	D 16-16
Italy	L 16-24

Played 3 Drawn 1 Lost 2

ARGENTINA TO EUROPE
NOVEMBER 2010

Opponents	Results
Italy	W 22-16
France	L 9-15
Ireland	L 9-29

Played 3 Won 1 Lost 2

OTHER INTERNATIONAL MATCH

Australia 26 New Zealand 24
(Bledisloe Cup; held in October in Hong Kong)

ROYAL BANK OF SCOTLAND
SIX NATIONS CHAMPIONSHIP 2011

Results			
Wales	19	England	26
Italy	11	Ireland	13
France	34	Scotland	21
England	59	Italy	13
Scotland	6	Wales	24
Ireland	22	France	25
Italy	16	Wales	24
England	17	France	9
Scotland	18	Ireland	21
Italy	22	France	21
Wales	19	Ireland	13
England	22	Scotland	16
Scotland	21	Italy	8
Ireland	24	England	8
France	28	Wales	9

Final Table

	P	W	D	L	F	A	PD	Pts
England	5	4	0	1	132	81	51	8
France	5	3	0	2	117	91	26	6
Ireland	5	3	0	2	93	81	12	6
Wales	5	3	0	2	95	89	6	6
Scotland	5	1	0	4	82	109	-27	2
Italy	5	1	0	4	70	138	-68	2

UNDER 20 SIX NATIONS 2011

Results

France	49	Scotland	5
Italy	9	Ireland	28
Wales	20	England	26
England	74	Italy	3
Scotland	3	Wales	33
Ireland	13	France	38
Italy	15	Wales	46
Scotland	0	Ireland	15
England	19	France	8
Italy	3	France	25
Wales	26	Ireland	26
England	56	Scotland	8
France	29	Wales	22
Scotland	7	Italy	9
Ireland	15	England	46

Final Table

	P	W	D	L	F	A	PD	Pts
England	5	5	0	0	221	54	167	10
France	5	4	0	1	149	62	87	8
Wales	5	2	1	2	147	99	48	5
Ireland	5	2	1	2	97	119	-22	5
Italy	5	1	0	4	39	180	-141	2
Scotland	5	0	0	5	23	162	-139	0

WOMEN'S SIX NATIONS 2011

Results

France	53	Scotland	3
Italy	5	Ireland	26
Wales	0	England	19
Ireland	12	France	14
England	68	Italy	5
Scotland	12	Wales	41
Scotland	5	Ireland	22
England	16	France	3
Italy	12	Wales	8
Italy	20	France	28
Wales	15	Ireland	14
England	89	Scotland	0
Ireland	0	England	31
France	15	Wales	0
Scotland	0	Italy	26

Final Table

	P	W	D	L	F	A	PD	Pts
England	5	5	0	0	223	8	215	10
France	5	4	0	1	113	51	62	8
Ireland	5	2	0	3	74	70	4	4
Wales	5	2	0	3	64	72	-8	4
Italy	5	2	0	3	68	130	-62	4
Scotland	5	0	0	5	20	231	-211	0

UNDER 18 SIX NATIONS

Results

Ireland	12	England	29
France	34	Italy	12
Wales	17	France	34
Italy	12	Wales	26
England	21	Scotland	26
Scotland	12	Ireland	31

TRI-NATIONS 2010

Results

New Zealand	32	South Africa	12
New Zealand	31	South Africa	17
Australia	30	South Africa	13
Australia	28	New Zealand	49
New Zealand	20	Australia	10
South Africa	22	New Zealand	29
South Africa	44	Australia	31
South Africa	39	Australia	41
Australia	22	New Zealand	23

Champions: New Zealand

TRI-NATIONS 2011

Results

Australia	39	South Africa	20
New Zealand	40	South Africa	7
New Zealand	30	Australia	14
South Africa	9	Australia	14
South Africa	18	New Zealand	5
Australia	25	New Zealand	20

Champions: Australia

* Due to the upcoming RWC, the Tri-Nations 2011 was limited to two rounds, home and away

IRB PACIFIC NATIONS CUP 2011

(Held in July in Fiji)

Tonga	45	Fiji	21
Japan	15	Samoa	34
Tonga	27	Japan	28
Samoa	18	Fiji	36
Tonga	29	Samoa	19
Japan	24	Fiji	13

Champions: Japan

CHURCHILL CUP 2011

(Held in June in Northampton, Esher, Gloucester and Worcester, England)

Pool A

USA	8	England Saxons	87
USA	13	Tonga	44
Tonga	14	England Saxons	41

Pool B

Canada	26	Italy A	12
Canada	34	Russia	18
Russia	19	Italy A	24

Bowl Final

USA	32	Russia	25

Plate Final

Tonga	18	Italy A	27

Final

England Saxons	37	Canada	6

* This was the last Churchill Cup competition.

100%
ENGLISH
BREWED IN BURY ST EDMUNDS SINCE 1799

GREENE KING IPA

OFFICIAL BEER
OF
ENGLAND
RUGBY

ENGLAND
RUGBY

A PROPER PINT
properpint.co.uk Enjoy responsibly

IRB NATIONS CUP 2011

(Held in June in Bucharest, Romania)

Romania	13	Namibia	11
Georgia	17	South African Kings	31
Argentina Jaguars	21	Portugal	25
Georgia	14	Argentina Jaguars	13
Romania	23	South African Kings	27
Portugal	23	Namibia	29
Portugal	12	South African Kings	39
Georgia	23	Namibia	18
Romania	13	Argentina Jaguars	37

Champions: South African Kings
Runners-up: Georgia

IRB JUNIOR WORLD CHAMPIONSHIP 2011

(Held in June in Italy)

Semi-finals
England	33	France	18
New Zealand	37	Australia	7

Third-place Play-off
France	17	Australia	30

Final
England	22	New Zealand	33

IRB JUNIOR WORLD RUGBY TROPHY 2011

(Held in May and June in Georgia)

Third-place Play-off
Uruguay	15	Georgia	20

Final
Samoa	31	Japan	24

WOMEN'S RUGBY WORLD CUP 2010

(Held in August and September in England)

Semi-finals
New Zealand	45	France	7
England	15	Australia	0

Third-place Play-off
France	8	Australia	22

Final
New Zealand	13	England	10

UNDER 18 EUROPEAN CHAMPIONSHIP 2011 (ELITE GROUP)

(Held in April in France)

Semi-finals
France	17	Ireland	19
England	38	Wales	34

Third-place Play-off
France	6	Wales	15

Final
Ireland	17	England	8

HSBC SEVENS WORLD SERIES FINALS 2010-11

Dubai
Samoa	21	England	29

South Africa (George)
England	19	New Zealand	22

New Zealand (Wellington)
England	14	New Zealand	29

United States (Las Vegas)
South Africa	24	Fiji	14

Hong Kong
New Zealand	29	England	17

Australia (Adelaide)
New Zealand	28	South Africa	20

England (Twickenham)
Fiji	14	South Africa	24

Scotland (Murrayfield)
Australia	35	South Africa	36

Champions: New Zealand

CLUB, COUNTY AND DIVISIONAL RUGBY

ENGLAND

Aviva Premiership

	P	W	D	L	F	A	BP	Pts
Leicester	22	16	1	5	594	403	12	78
Saracens	22	18	0	4	484	318	4	76
Gloucester	22	14	1	7	528	452	9	67
Northampton	22	14	0	8	533	430	9	65
Bath	22	13	1	8	427	367	8	62
London Irish	22	11	0	11	523	459	10	54
Harlequins	22	9	2	11	482	384	12	52
*Exeter	22	10	0	12	428	460	5	43
London Wasps	22	9	1	12	425	497	5	43
Sale	22	6	1	15	432	618	6	32
Newcastle	22	4	1	17	360	553	5	23
Leeds	22	4	0	18	315	590	7	23

*Exeter deducted two points for fielding an ineligible player.

Relegated: Leeds

Aviva Premiership Play-offs

Semi-finals

Leicester	11	Northampton	3
Saracens	12	Gloucester	10

Final

Leicester	18	Saracens	22

RFU National Championship
Play-Off Winners: Worcester
Play-Off Runners-up: Cornish Pirates

Promoted to Premiership: Worcester

National Leagues
National 1 Champions: London Scottish
Runners-up: Barking
National 2 (S) Champions: Ealing Trailfinders
Runners-up: Jersey
National 2 (N) Champions: Fylde
Runners-up: Loughborough Students

Note: The RFU cancelled the National League Cup competitions because of a backlog of fixtures due to the adverse weather conditions.

RFU Knockout Trophy Finals

Intermediate Cup

Stoke-on-Trent	16	Aylesford Bulls	10

Senior Vase

Littleborough	8	Teddington	42

Junior Vase

HAC	37	Edwardians	6

National Under 20 Championship Final

Gloucestershire	62	Hampshire	30

County Championship Finals

Bill Beaumont Cup

Hertfordshire	23	Lancashire	32

County Championship Shield

Surrey	22	Dorset & Wilts	43

Bill Beaumont Cup Division Two (Plate)

Northumberland	31	North Midlands	17

Oxbridge University Matches

Varsity Match

Oxford	21	Cambridge	10

Under 21 Varsity Match

Cambridge	20	Oxford	5

Women's Varsity Match

Cambridge	22	Oxford	0

BUCS Competitions
Men's Championship Winners: Durham
Women's C'ship Winners: Exeter
Men's Trophy Winners: Nottingham Trent
Women's Trophy Winners: Bath

Inter-Services Champions: Army

Hospitals Cup Winners: Imperial Medics

Middlesex Sevens 2010
Winners: ULR Samurai International
Runners-up: London Irish

Rosslyn Park Schools Sevens
Open Winners: Filton College
Festival Winners: Wellington College
Colts Winners: Tonbridge
Preparatory Winners: Bromsgrove
Juniors Winners: London Oratory
Girls Winners: Hartpury College

Daily Mail Schools Day
Under 18 Cup Winners: Whitgift School
Under 18 Vase Winners: Solihull School
Under 15 Cup Winners: RGS High Wycombe
Under 15 Vase Winners: Saffron Walden CHS

RFUW Premiership Champions: Richmond

SCOTLAND

Premier Cup Final
Melrose   21   Ayr   25

National Shield Final
Lasswade   22   Hawick YM   17

Regional Bowl Final
Duns   30   Strathendrick   6

Scottish Sevens Winners
Kelso: Melrose
Selkirk: Selkirk
Melrose: Melrose
Hawick: Hawick
Berwick: Jed-Forest
Langholm: Jed-Forest
Peebles: Peebles
Gala: Melrose
Earlston: Melrose
Jed-Forest: Melrose
Kings of the Sevens: Melrose

Scottish Premiership
Division 1

	P	W	D	L	F	A	BP	Pts
Melrose	11	9	0	2	361	239	10	46
Glasgow	11	9	1	1	375	174	7	45
Ayr	11	9	0	2	345	202	8	44
Heriot's	11	8	0	3	320	243	6	38
Currie	11	5	3	3	317	247	10	36
Dundee	11	5	1	5	432	302	12	34
Boroughmuir	11	6	0	5	260	271	6	30
Hawick	11	4	0	7	252	219	10	26
Stirling	11	4	0	7	281	336	5	21
West of Scotland	11	2	1	8	257	497	6	16
Watsonians	11	1	0	10	208	391	3	7
Selkirk	11	1	0	10	168	455	3	7

Champions: Melrose
Relegated: Watsonians, Selkirk

Division 2

	P	W	D	L	F	A	BP	Pts
Edinburgh Acads	11	10	0	1	331	200	7	47
Gala	11	9	1	1	296	190	5	43
Aberdeen	11	8	1	2	340	217	7	41
Peebles	11	7	1	3	243	215	3	33
Jed-Forest	11	5	1	5	275	241	8	30
Hillhead/J'hill	11	6	0	5	294	275	6	30
Falkirk	11	5	1	5	289	300	8	30
Biggar	11	4	0	7	276	310	5	21
Stewart's Melville	11	3	0	8	261	356	4	16
Kirkcaldy	11	2	1	8	227	299	5	15
Kelso	11	2	0	9	215	319	5	13
GHA	11	2	0	9	197	322	4	12

Champions: Edinburgh Academicals
Also promoted: Gala
Relegated: GHA

WALES

SWALEC Cup
Semi-finals
Llandovery   12   Aberavon   18
Pontypridd   33   Swansea   22

Final
Aberavon   24   Pontypridd   35

SWALEC Plate Final
Ammanford   35   Glynneath   13

SWALEC Bowl Final
Maesteg Harlequins 18   Senghenydd   28

Principality Premiership

	P	W	D	L	F	A	BP	Pts
Pontypridd	26	23	1	2	767	382	13	107
Neath	26	21	0	5	733	426	16	100
Llanelli	26	19	0	7	869	586	15	91
Aberavon	26	17	0	9	814	633	15	83
Swansea	26	12	1	13	761	670	22	72
Cross Keys	26	13	1	12	636	543	14	68
Newport	26	14	1	11	620	657	8	66
Tonmawr	26	12	2	12	614	651	13	65
Cardiff Rugby	26	10	2	14	611	613	15	59
Bedwas	26	11	0	15	517	666	10	54
Carmarthen	26	9	0	17	518	710	7	43
Pontypool	26	7	1	18	584	721	8	38
Llandovery	26	6	1	19	511	719	12	38
Wanderers	26	3	0	23	489	1067	9	21

SWALEC Leagues

Division 1 East Champions: Ebbw Vale
Runners-up: Newbridge
Division 1 West Champions: Bridgend
Runners-up: Narberth
Division 1 North Champions: Caernarfon
Runners-up: Nant Conwy

Division 2 East Champions: Mountain Ash
Runners-up: Tredegar
Division 2 West Champions: Ammanford
Runners-up: Tondu
Division 2 North Champions: Bala
Runners-up: Llanidloes

Division 3 East Champions: Rhymney
Runners-up: Garndiffaith
Division 3 Southeast Champions: Abercynon
Runners-up: Heol y Cyw
Division 3 Southwest Champions: Glynneath
Runners-up: Kenfig Hill
Division 3 West Champions: Crymych
Runners-up: Mumbles
Division 3 North Champions: Menai Bridge
Runners-up: Rhosllanerchrugog

IRELAND

Ulster Bank League
Division 1A

	P	W	D	L	F	A	BP	Pts
Cork Const'n	14	10	2	2	275	179	3	47
Old Belvedere	14	9	1	4	279	197	6	44
Young Munster	14	8	0	6	220	197	5	37
St Mary's Coll	14	7	0	7	278	224	7	35
Blackrock Coll	14	6	0	8	267	304	4	28
Dolphin	14	5	1	8	221	274	4	26
Shannon	14	5	0	9	225	327	6	26
Garryowen	14	3	2	9	204	267	6	22

Division 1B

	P	W	D	L	F	A	BP	Pts
Clontarf	14	10	0	4	310	213	7	47
Lansdowne	14	7	0	7	356	225	12	40
Buccaneers	14	7	0	7	274	221	8	36
UL Bohemian	14	7	0	7	259	276	5	33
Dungannon	14	7	0	7	284	341	4	32
UCC	14	6	0	8	235	316	5	29
Galwegians	14	6	0	8	239	309	4	28
Bruff	14	6	0	8	219	275	1	25

Ulster Bank League Play-offs
Division 1

Semi-finals

Old Belvedere	22	Clontarf	20
Cork Constitution	19	Young Munster	9

Final

Old Belvedere	20	Cork Constitution	17

Division 1 Play-off

Garryowen	23	Buccaneers	9

(Garryowen stay in Division 1A; Buccaneers stay in Division 1B)

Division 2
Champions: Ballynahinch
Runners-up: UCD

Division 2 Play-off

Bruff	25	Bective Rangers	12

(Bruff stay in Division 1B; Bective Rangers will be in Division 2A)

Division 3
Champions: City of Derry
Runners-up: Seapoint

Division 3 Play-off

Old Crescent	16	Banbridge	15

(Old Crescent will be in Division 2A; Banbridge will be in Division 2B)

All Ireland Cup Final

Bruff	24	Dungannon	18

All Ireland Junior Cup Final

Crosshaven	17	Monivea	9

MAGNERS LEAGUE 2010-11

	P	W	D	L	F	A	BP	Pts
Munster	22	19	0	3	496	327	7	83
Leinster	22	15	1	6	495	336	8	70
Ulster	22	15	1	6	480	418	5	67
Ospreys	22	12	1	9	553	418	13	63
Scarlets	22	12	1	9	503	453	12	62
Blues	22	13	1	8	479	392	6	60
Dragons	22	10	1	11	444	462	7	49
Edinburgh	22	9	0	13	421	460	7	43
Connacht	22	7	1	14	394	459	9	39
Treviso	22	9	0	13	374	502	2	38
Glasgow	22	6	1	15	401	543	7	33
Aironi	22	1	0	21	247	517	8	12

Magners League Play-offs
Semi-finals

Munster	18	Ospreys	11
Leinster	18	Ulster	3

Final

Munster	19	Leinster	9

LV= CUP 2010-11

Semi-finals

Gloucester	45	Dragons	17
Harlequins	20	Newcastle Falcons	21

Final

Gloucester	34	Newcastle Falcons	7

BRITISH & IRISH CUP 2010-11

Final

Bristol	17	Bedford Blues	14

FRANCE

'Top 14' Play-offs

Semi-finals

Toulouse	29	Clermont A'gne	6
Racing Métro	25	Montpellier	26

Final

Toulouse	15	Montpellier	10

ITALY

'Super 10'

Final

Rovigo	14	Petrarca Padova	18

HEINEKEN CUP 2010-11

Quarter-finals

Perpignan	29	Toulon	25
Leinster	17	Leicester	10
Northampton	23	Ulster	13
Biarritz	20	Toulouse	27

Semi-finals

Leinster	32	Toulouse	23
Northampton	23	Perpignan	7

Final

Leinster	33	Northampton	22

AMLIN CHALLENGE CUP 2010-11

Quarter-finals

La Rochelle	13	Clermont A'gne	23
Harlequins	32	London Wasps	22
Stade Français	32	Montpellier	28
Brive	37	Munster	42

Semi-finals

Stade Français	29	Clermont A'gne	25
Munster	12	Harlequins	20

Final

Harlequins	19	Stade Français	18

NEW ZEALAND

ITM Cup 2010

Final

Canterbury	33	Waikato	13

Ranfurly Shield holders: Southland

SOUTH AFRICA

Currie Cup 2010

Final

Natal Sharks	30	Western Province	10

SUPER 15 2011

Final Table

	P	W	D	L	F	A	BP	Pts
Reds	16	13	0	3	429	309	6	66
Stormers	16	12	0	4	400	257	7	63
Crusaders	16	11	1	4	436	273	7	61
Blues	16	10	1	5	405	335	10	60
Waratahs	16	10	0	6	398	252	9	57
Sharks	16	10	1	5	407	339	7	57
Bulls	16	10	0	6	416	370	6	54
Highlanders	16	8	0	8	296	343	5	45
Hurricanes	16	5	2	9	328	398	10	42
Chiefs	16	6	1	9	332	348	6	40
Cheetahs	16	5	0	11	435	437	12	40
Western Force	16	5	2	9	333	416	5	37
Brumbies	16	4	1	11	314	437	7	33
Lions	16	3	1	12	351	477	7	29
M'bourne Rebels	16	3	0	13	281	570	4	24

Semi-finals

Reds	30	Blues	13
Crusaders	29	Stormers	10

Final

Reds	18	Crusaders	13

BARBARIANS

Opponents	Results
Combined Services	W 46-21
South Africa	W 26-20
Richmond	W 45-36
Bedford Blues	W 43-35
England	W 38-32
Wales	W 31-28

Played 6, Won 6

**Proud to support
Wooden Spoon**

PREVIEW OF THE
SEASON 2011-12

Key Players

selected by IAN ROBERTSON

ENGLAND

CHRIS ASHTON
Northampton Saints
Born: 29 March 1987
Height: 6ft Weight: 14st 6lbs
Wing – 12 caps
1st cap v France 2010

COURTNEY LAWES
Northampton Saints
Born: 23 February 1989
Height: 6ft 7ins Weight: 18st
Lock/Back-row – 8 caps
1st cap v Australia 2009

SCOTLAND

RUARIDH JACKSON
Glasgow Warriors
Born: 12 February 1988
Height: 6ft Weight: 13st 9lbs
Fly half – 7 caps
1st cap v New Zealand 2010

RICHIE GRAY
Glasgow Warriors
Born: 24 August 1989
Height: 6ft 10ins Weight: 20st 5lbs
Lock – 11 caps
1st cap v France 2010

WALES

GEORGE NORTH
Scarlets
Born: 13 April 1992
Height: 6ft 3ins Weight: 15st 3lbs
Wing/Centre – 6 caps
1st cap v South Africa 2010

SAM WARBURTON
Cardiff Blues
Born: 5 October 1988
Height: 6ft 2ins Weight: 15st 8lbs
Back-row – 16 caps
1st cap v USA 2009

Six Nations Championship

2011-12

IRELAND

JONATHAN SEXTON
Leinster
Born: 11 July 1985
Height: 6ft 2ins Weight: 14st 6lbs
Fly half – 17 caps
1st cap v Fiji 2009

DENIS LEAMY
Munster
Born: 27 November 1981
Height: 6ft 2ins Weight: 16st 13lbs
Back-row – 51 caps
1st cap v USA 2004

FRANCE

MAXIME MEDARD
Stade Toulousain
Born: 16 November 1986
Height: 5ft 11ins Weight: 13st 11lbs
Full back/Wing – 19 caps
1st cap v Argentina 2008

LIONEL NALLET
Racing Métro 92
Born: 14 September 1976
Height: 6ft 5ins Weight: 18st
Lock – 62 caps
1st cap v Romania 2000

ITALY

LUKE McLEAN
Treviso
Born: 26 June 1987
Height: 6ft 3ins Weight: 15st 3lbs
Full back/Fly half – 28 caps
1st cap v South Africa 2008

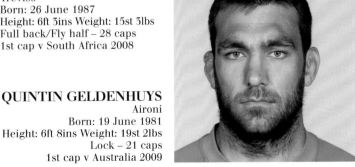

QUINTIN GELDENHUYS
Aironi
Born: 19 June 1981
Height: 6ft 8ins Weight: 19st 2lbs
Lock – 21 caps
1st cap v Australia 2009

Fixtures 2011-12

JULY 2011

Sat. 23rd	AUSTRALIA v SA (Tri-Nations)
Sat. 30th	NZ v SA (Tri-Nations)

AUGUST 2011

Sat. 6th	ENGLAND v WALES (w-u)
	SCOTLAND v IRELAND (w-u)
	NZ v AUSTRALIA (Tri-Nations)
Sat. 13th	WALES v ENGLAND (w-u)
	FRANCE v IRELAND (w-u)
	SA v AUSTRALIA (Tri-Nations)
Sat. 20th	IRELAND v FRANCE (w-u)
	WALES v ARGENTINA (w-u)
	SCOTLAND v ITALY (w-u)
	SA v NZ (Tri-Nations)
	RBS Scottish Premiership 1, 2
Sat. 27th	IRELAND v ENGLAND (w-u)
	English National Leagues
	RBS Scottish Premiership 1-3
	RBS Scottish National Lge 1
	Welsh Principality Premiership

SEPTEMBER 2011

Fri. 2nd to	
Sun. 4th	Rabo Direct PRO12
Sat. 3rd	English National Leagues
	RBS Scottish Premiership 1-3
	RBS Scottish National Lge 1
	Welsh Principality Premiership
	Swalec Welsh National Lges
Sat. 3rd and	
Sun. 4th	Aviva English Premiership
	English National Championship
Fri. 9th to	
Sun. 11th	Aviva English Premiership
	Rabo Direct PRO12
Sat. 10th	English National Leagues
	RBS Scottish Premiership 1-3
	RBS Scottish National Lge 1
	Welsh Principality Premiership
	Swalec Welsh National Lges
Sat. 10th and	
Sun. 11th	English National Championship
Fri. 16th to	
Sun. 18th	English National Championship
	Rabo Direct PRO12
Sat. 17th	English National Leagues
	RBS Scottish Premiership 1-3
	RBS Scottish National Lge 1
	Welsh Principality Premiership
	Swalec Welsh National Lges
Sat. 17th and	
Sun. 18th	Aviva English Premiership
Wed. 21st	British & Irish Cup (part Rd 1)
Fri. 23rd to	
to Sun. 25th	Aviva English Premiership
	Rabo Direct PRO12

Sat. 24th	English National Leagues
	RBS Scottish Premiership 1-3
	RBS Scottish National Lge 1
	Welsh Principality Premiership
	Swalec Welsh National Lges
Sat. 24th and	
Sun. 25th	English National Championship

OCTOBER 2011

Fri. 30th Sept. to	
Sun. 2nd Oct.	Aviva English Premiership
	English National Championship
	Rabo Direct PRO12
Sat. 1st	English National Leagues
	RBS Scottish Premiership 1-3
	RBS Scottish National Lge 1
	Welsh Principality Premiership
	Swalec Welsh National Lges
	UB Irish Leagues 1A/B, 2A/B
Fri. 7th and	
Sat. 8th	English National Championship
	UB Irish Leagues 1A/B, 2A/B
Fri. 7th to	
Sun. 9th	Aviva English Premiership
	Rabo Direct PRO12
	Heineken Cup (1)
Sat. 8th	English National Leagues
	RBS Scottish Premiership 1-3
	RBS Scottish National Lge 1
	Welsh Principality Premiership
Weds. 12th	British & Irish Cup (part Rd 1)
Fri. 14th &	
Sat. 15th	UB Irish Leagues 1A/B, 2A/B
Fri. 14th to	
Sun. 16th	English National Championship
	LV= Anglo-Welsh Cup (1)
	Heineken Cup (2)
Sat. 15th	English National Leagues
	RBS Scottish Premiership 1-3
	RBS Scottish National Lge 1
	Welsh Principality Premiership
	Swalec Welsh National Lges
Fri.21st to	
Sun. 23rd	English National Championship
	LV= Anglo-Welsh Cup (2)
Sat. 22nd	English National Leagues
	RBS Scottish Premiership 1-3
	RBS Scottish National Lge 1
	Welsh Principality Premiership
	Swalec Welsh National Lges
Fri. 28th and	
Sat. 29th	Aviva English Premiership
	English National Championship
	UB Irish Leagues 1A/B, 2A/B
Fri. 28th to	
Sun. 30th	Rabo Direct PRO12
Sat. 29th	English National Leagues

RBS Scottish Premiership 1-3
Welsh Principality Premiership
Swalec Welsh National Lges

NOVEMBER 2011

Fri. 4th and Sat. 5th	UB Irish Leagues 1A/B, 2A/B
Fri. 4th to Sun. 6th	Aviva English Premiership Rabo Direct PRO12
Sat. 5th	English National Leagues RBS Scottish Premiership 1-3 RBS Scottish National Lge 1 Welsh Principality Premiership
Sat. 5th and Sun. 6th	English National Championship
Thu. 10th to Sun. 13th	Amlin Challenge Cup (1)
Sat. 12th	English National Leagues RBS Scottish Premiership 3 RBS Scottish National Lge 1 Welsh Principality Premiership Swalec Welsh National Lges
Sat. 12th and Sun. 13th	British & Irish Cup (2)
Thu. 17th to Sun. 20th	Amlin Challenge Cup (2)
Sat. 19th	English National Leagues RBS Scottish Premiership 3 RBS Scottish National Lge 1 Welsh Principality Premiership Swalec Welsh National Lges British & Irish Cup (part Rd 3)
Sat. 19th and Sun. 20th	English National Championship
Fri. 25th and Sat. 26th	English National Championship UB Irish Leagues 1A/B, 2A/B
Fri. 25th to Sun. 27th	Aviva English Premiership Rabo Direct PRO12
Sat. 26th	Barbarians v Australia English National Leagues RBS Scottish Premiership 3 RBS Scottish National Lge 1 Welsh Principality Premiership Swalec Welsh National Lges

DECEMBER 2011

Fri. 2nd to Sun. 4th	Aviva English Premiership English National Championship Rabo Direct PRO12
Sat. 3rd	N HEMISPHERE v S HEMISPHERE (Heroes Rugby Challenge – Twickenham) English National Leagues RBS Scottish National Lge 1 Welsh Principality Premiership UB Irish Leagues 1A/B, 2A/B
Thu. 8th	Oxford U v Cambridge U (Twickenham)
Thu. 8th to Sun. 11th	Amlin Challenge Cup (3)
Fri. 9th to Sun. 11th	Heineken Cup (3)
Sat. 10th	English National Championship English National Leagues RBS Scottish National Lge 1 Welsh Principality Premiership Swalec Cup (1) British & Irish Cup (part Rd 3)
Thu. 15th to Sun. 18th	Amlin Challenge Cup (4)
Fri. 16th to Sun. 18th	Heineken Cup (4)
Sat. 17th	English National Leagues RBS Scottish Premiership 3 RBS Scottish National Lge 1 Welsh Principality Premiership Swalec Welsh National Lges British & Irish Cup (4)
Fri. 23rd and Sat. 24th	Rabo Direct PRO12
Sat. 24th to Mon. 26th	Aviva English Premiership English National Championship
Mon. 26th	Welsh Principality Premiership
Fri. 30th to Sun. 1st Jan.	English National Championship Rabo Direct PRO12
Sat. 31st	Aviva English Premiership Swalec Welsh National Lges

JANUARY 2012

Mon. 2nd	Welsh Principality Premiership
Fri. 6th and Sat. 7th	UB Irish Leagues 1A/B
Fri. 6th to Sun. 8th	Aviva English Premiership Rabo Direct PRO12
Sat. 7th	English National Leagues Welsh Principality Premiership Swalec Welsh National Lges
Sat. 7th and Sun. 8th	English National Championship
Mon. 9th and Tue. 10th	UB Irish Leagues 2A/B
Thu. 12th to Sun. 15th	Amlin Challenge Cup (5)
Fri. 13th and Sat. 14th	UB Irish Leagues 1A/B, 2B
Fri. 13th to Sun. 15th	Heineken Cup (5)
Sat. 14th	English National Leagues RBS Scottish Premiership 1-3 RBS Scottish National Lge 1 Welsh Principality Premiership Swalec Welsh National Lges
Sat. 14th and Sun. 15th	English National Championship

Thu. 19th to Sun. 22nd	Amlin Challenge Cup (6)
Fri. 20th to Sun. 22nd	Heineken Cup (6)
Sat. 21st	English National Leagues
	RBS Scottish National Lge 1
	Welsh Principality Premiership
	Swalec Welsh National Lges
	British & Irish Cup q/finals
Fri. 27th to Sun. 29th	LV= Anglo-Welsh Cup (3)
Sat. 28th	English National Leagues
	RBS Scottish Premiership 1-3
	RBS Scottish National Lge 1
	Swalec Welsh National Lges
	Swalec Cup (2)
	UB Irish Leagues 1A/B, 2A/B
Sat. 28th and Sun. 29th	English National Championship

FEBRUARY 2012

Fri. 3rd and Sat. 4th	UB Irish Leagues 1A/B, 2A/B
Fri. 3rd to Sun. 5th	English National Championship
	LV= Anglo-Welsh Cup (4)
Sat. 4th	FRANCE v ITALY (14:30)
	SCOTLAND v ENGLAND (17:00)
	English National Championship
	Welsh Principality Premiership
Sun. 5th	IRELAND v WALES (15:00)
Fri. 10th and Sat. 11th	UB Irish Leagues 1A/B
Fri. 10th to Sun. 12th	Aviva English Premiership
	Rabo Direct PRO12
Sat. 11th	ITALY v ENGLAND (16:00)
	FRANCE v IRELAND (20:00)
	English National Leagues
	RBS Scottish Premiership 1
	RBS Scottish National Lge 1
	Welsh Principality Premiership
	Swalec Welsh National Lges
Sun. 12th	WALES v SCOTLAND (15:00)
Fri. 17th and Sat. 18th	UB Irish Leagues 1A/B, 2A/B
Fri. 17th to Sun. 19th	Aviva English Premiership
	Rabo Direct PRO12
Sat. 18th	English National Leagues
	RBS Scottish Premiership 1-3
	RBS Scottish National Lge 1
	Swalec Welsh National Lges
	Swalec Cup (3)
Sat. 18th and Sun. 19th	English National Championship
Fri. 24th to Sun. 26th	Aviva English Premiership
	Rabo Direct PRO12
Sat. 25th	IRELAND v ITALY (13:30)
	ENGLAND v WALES (16:00)
	English National Championship

Sun. 26th	Welsh Principality Premiership
	SCOTLAND v FRANCE (15:00)

MARCH 2012

Fri. 2nd and Sat. 3rd	UB Irish Leagues 1A/B, 2A/B
Fri. 2nd to Sun. 4th	Aviva English Premiership
	Rabo Direct PRO12
Sat. 3rd	English National Leagues
	RBS Scottish Premiership 1-3
	RBS Scottish National Lge 1
	Welsh Principality Premiership
	Swalec Welsh National Lges
Fri. 9th	Welsh Principality Premiership
Fri. 9th to Sun. 11th	LV= Anglo-Welsh Cup s/finals•
Sat. 10th	WALES v ITALY (14:30)
	IRELAND v SCOTLAND (17:00)
	English National Championship
	Pool Play-off (1)
	English National Leagues
	RBS Scottish National Lge 1
	Welsh Principality Premiership
Sun. 11th	FRANCE v ENGLAND (15:00)
Fri. 16th	Welsh Principality Premiership
Fri. 16th to Sun. 18th	LV= Anglo-Welsh Cup final•
Sat. 17th	ITALY v SCOTLAND (12:30)
	WALES v FRANCE (14:45)
	ENGLAND v IRELAND (17:00)
	English National Championship
	Pool Play-off (2)
	RBS Scottish Premiership 1-3
Fri. 23rd and Sat. 24th	UB Irish Leagues 1A/B, 2A/B
Fri. 23rd to Sun. 25th	Aviva English Premiership
	Rabo Direct PRO12
Sat. 24th	English National Leagues
	English National Championship
	Pool Play-off (3)
	Swalec Welsh National Lges
	Swalec Cup (4)
	RBS Scottish Premiership 1-3
Wed. 28th	BUCS finals (Twickenham)
Fri. 30th and Sat. 31st	UB Irish Leagues 1A/B, 2A/B
Fri. 30th to Sun. 1st Apr.	Aviva English Premiership
	Rabo Direct PRO12
Sat. 31st	English National Leagues
	English National Championship
	Pool Play-off (4)
	Swalec Welsh National Lges

APRIL 2012

Wed. 4th	Daily Mail RBS Schools Day
Fri. 6th to Sun. 8th	Heineken Cup quarter-finals
	Amlin Challenge Cup q/finals
Sat. 7th	Welsh Principality Premiership

	Swalec Welsh National Lges
	British & Irish Cup semi-finals
Fri. 13th and Sat. 14th	Aviva English Premiership
Fri. 13th to Sun. 15th	Rabo Direct PRO12
Sat. 14th	English National Leagues
	English National Championship Pool Play-off (5)
	Welsh Principality Premiership
	Swalec Welsh National Lges
	Swalec Cup semi-finals
	Swalec Plate semi-finals
	Swalec Bowl semi-finals
	UB Irish Leagues 1A/B, 2A/B
Fri. 20th and Sat. 21st	Aviva English Premiership
Fri. 20th to Sun. 22nd	Rabo Direct PRO12
Sat. 21st	English National Championship Pool Play-off (6)
	English National Leagues
	RBS Scottish Premier Cup final
	RBS Scottish Shield final
	RBS Scottish Bowl final
	Swalec Welsh National Lges
	UB Irish Leagues 1A/B
Fri. 27th to Sun. 29th	Amlin Challenge Cup s/finals•
Sat. 28th	Army v Navy – Babcock Trophy
	Combined Services U23 v Oxbridge U23 (both Twickenham)
	English National Leagues
	Swalec Welsh National Lges
	British & Irish Cup final
Sat. 28th and Sun. 29th	Heineken Cup semi-finals•
Mon. 30th	Aviva 'A' League final

MAY 2012

Fri. 4th to Sun. 6th	Rabo Direct PRO12
Sat. 5th	Aviva English Premiership
	English National Championship Play-off semi-finals (1)
	Welsh Principality Premiership Play-off Round 1
	U20 Championship final
	RFU Intermediate Cup final
	RFU Senior Vase final
	RFU Junior Vase final
Sat. 12th	English National Championship Play-off semi-finals (2)
	Swalec Cup final•
	Swalec Plate final•
	Swalec Bowl final•
Sat. 12th and Sun. 13th	Emirates Airline London 7s
	Aviva English Premiership semi-finals
	Rabo Direct PRO12 s/finals•
Fri. 18th to Sun. 20th	Heineken Cup final•
	Amlin Challenge Cup final•
Sat. 19th	English National Championship Play-off final (1)
	Welsh Principality Premiership Play-off finals
Sat. 26th	Aviva English Premiership final
	Rabo Direct PRO12 final•
	Barbarians v England Saxons
	English National Championship Play-off final (2)
Sun. 27th	Bill Beaumont Cup final
	County Championship Shield final

Notes
1. (w-u) indicates RWC 2011 warm-up match
2. • indicates dates and times to be confirmed

Here's your chance to create a stir for disadvantaged children in the UK and Ireland.

Join Wooden Spoon, the childrens' charity of rugby, to help disadvantaged children and young people throughout the UK and Ireland.

Every year Wooden Spoon's members have great fun participating in a wide variety of adventures and events which raise money to provide assistance to youngsters whose circumstances are so much more difficult than our own.

Visit www.woodenspoon.com to see the many ways in which you can take part in delivering real, tangible improvements to the lives of many thousands of appreciative kids.

Membership costs just £40 per year. To apply for membership simply email members@woodenspoon.com

Donate: If membership isn't your thing, you can still make a donation by texting "SPOON" to 70700*.

www.woodenspoon.com

Wooden Spoon, 41 Frimley High St, Frimley, Surrey, GU16 7HJ
Charity Registration No. 326691 Scotland No: SC039247

Wooden Spoon
The children's charity of rugby

* A donation will cost £5 plus the cost of the text from your mobile operator.
The minimum the charity will receive from your donation is £4.51